MITCHELL BEAZLEY
DISCOVERING WINE COUNTRY

Northern Spain

Susie Barrie

Series editor: Patrick Matthews

DISCOVERING WINE COUNTRY
NORTHERN SPAIN
by Susie Barrie

First published in Great Britain in 2006
by Mitchell Beazley, an imprint of Octopus Publishing Group Ltd,
2–4 Heron Quays, London E14 4JP.

A CIP catalogue record for this book is available from the British Library.

ISBN: 1 84533 133 8

The author and publishers will be grateful for any information which will assist them in keeping
future editions up to date. Although all reasonable care has been taken in the preparation of this
book, neither the publishers nor the author can accept any liability for any consequences arising
from the use thereof, or the information contained therein.

Photographs by Tory McTernan
Map creation by Encompass Graphics

Commissioning Editor Hilary Lumsden
Executive Art Editor Yasia Williams-Leedham
Managing Editor Julie Sheppard
Editor Samantha Stokes
Designer Gaelle Lochner
Index Hilary Bird
Production Gary Hayes

Typeset in Futura and Sabon

Printed and bound by Toppan Printing Company in China

Contents

How to use this book

Discovering Wine Country is all about getting you from the page to the producer. Each chapter covers a specific winemaking region of interest, and includes a map of the area featured, with places of interest marked using the symbols below. The leading wine producers mentioned are all given a map grid reference so you can see exactly where they are.

The maps include key features to help you navigate your way round the routes, but they are not intended to replace detailed road maps, or indeed detailed vineyard maps, normally available from local tourist offices or the local wine bureau (*see* below right).

The locations of recommended wine producers are marked on the maps with the sign ♣ . The wine regions covered are packed with other points of interest for the wine enthusiast that are unrelated to actual wine purchasing. These are shown as ♯ . Sometimes this includes growers who don't sell direct but whose status is such that they will be on any wine-lover's itinerary. Recommended restaurants are marked ⭐OI and towns and villages where there's an Oficina de Turismo (tourist office) are marked ⓘ .

Quick reference map symbols

♣   recommended wine producer
♯   wine tourist site
★   tourist attraction
⭐OI   recommended restaurant
ⓘ   tourist information centre

▢▢▢▢   named wine region

═══════   author's suggested wine route(s) to follow, with information about how long the route is and any other useful tips

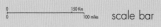   scale bar

   north compass

Boxed information

▬▬▬   the contact details of hotels, restaurants, tourist information, hire shops, transport facilities, and other points of interest

  wine-related information as well as the author's selection of the top growers to visit in the specific area featured, including contact details and a map reference

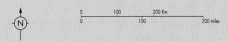

Atlantic Ocean

La Coruña
Oviedo
ASTURIAS
Santander
CANTABRIA
Bilbao
PAÍS
VASCO
FRANCE
GALICIA
León
Pamplona
NAVARRA
ANDORRA
Vigo
CASTILLA-LEÓN
LA RIOJA
Girona
CATALUÑA
Lleida
Valladolid
Zaragoza
A2
E80
E5
ARAGÓN
Barcelona
A6
PORTUGAL
Madrid
N234
A7
Valencia
Mérida
Albacete
A7
E5
Murcia
Sevilla
Cartagena
Granada
E15
Mediterranean Sea
Jerez
Málaga
Cádiz
Algeciras

Local wine bureaus:

www.ribeirasacra.org
www.do-ribeiro.com
www.riojawine.com
www.vinonavarra.com
www.do-conca.org

www.domontsant.com
www.doriasbaixas.com
www.getariakotxakolina.com
www.dosomontano.com
www.dopenedes.es

Introduction

A sk anyone the world over to name a Spanish wine and you can bet your granny's false teeth the response will be Rioja or cava. This isn't of course a bad thing. Both Rioja and cava come from traditional Spanish regions producing highly individual, often world-class wines and – unlike the faceless "creeks" and "valleys" that so often appear on wine labels today – they actually exist.

The time is now

What's incredible about Northern Spain is that Rioja and Catalonia (the home of most cava) are only the tip of the iceberg, and all the unknown regions between and beyond are just waiting to be discovered. With air travel costing less by the day and with the Spanish wine scene looking more exciting than ever, there couldn't be a better time to visit than right now.

So who is this book for? It's for people who love Spanish wine but have never visited its wine regions; it's for people who know they like Spain, but want to learn more about its wines; and it's for those who've simply always fancied going on a wine holiday but have never known where to start.

BELOW *The streets of Galicia's medieval capital, Santiago de Compostela, are perfect for an afternoon's stroll.*

Your own journey of discovery

To talk about "Northern Spain" is to talk about a vast area of land and, unlike say Burgundy or Bordeaux, it's not possible to travel all of its wine-producing areas in one go. What I hope is that this book will be a useful companion on your first wine holiday, and once you're hooked, you won't be able to resist the urge to return and discover more.

Each chapter in the second part of the book deals with a sizeable chunk of land, so you'll find that most of my suggested routes are relatively long, and include more bodegas than it's possible to visit in just one day. My motivation in doing this was firstly to make you aware of all the best bodegas and the style of wine they specialize in, giving you the opportunity to pick and choose according to your own taste. Secondly, I didn't want you to miss any of the wonderful landscape, the beautiful monasteries, the rural villages, or the hidden bodegas, and my intention was for you to break up most of the routes with an overnight stop in a recommended small hotel.

You'll find that along with tiny *garagiste*

bodegas, I've included slightly shabby old cooperatives, everyday family firms, and huge glamorous corporations with smart new visitor centres and endless rows of shiny stainless-steel tanks. This is because I firmly believe that in order to understand Spain and its wine industry fully, it's vital that you see the wine being made in as many ways as possible. It's also true to say that unlike Bordeaux, and in some ways Burgundy, the size and stature of a given winery don't automatically equate to the price of its wines. The fact is that you'll find some absolute bargains at the most imposing of bodegas, and by contrast, prices that'll make your jaw drop at the humblest of abodes.

Be bold

Whatever you do, don't be intimidated. If you don't ask, you'll never know, and you'd be amazed how happy winemakers can be to answer the most basic of queries. The first section of this book is intended to help of course, with lots of information on the various wines, how they're made, what you should expect when you visit a winery, the history of the people and their customs, and what to do when you're all wined out.

ABOVE *The region of Priorat was named after the 12th-century priory of Escala Dei.*

What you should never do is feel obliged to purchase wine, unless of course you've been given a free visit and tasting, in which case it's only polite to buy a bottle or two in return for your host's time. If you don't like the wines or feel they're too expensive, you can always use the excuse that you simply can't manage to carry any more bottles home. On the other hand, if you know immediately that a wine is to your taste, there's no greater compliment to a winemaker than to express an interest in buying his or her wine. Remember that above all you're the one who's going to be drinking it, so it doesn't matter if it's the most famous wine in the world, or a bottle that no one's ever heard of – if it does it for you that's all that counts.

Maps, guides, and spelling

This book is intended to be used alongside other maps and guides. Although I've included many cultural, culinary, and historical places across the huge region of Northern Spain, this is a book about visiting wineries, and should be used as such. The Michelin map and website (www.viamichelin.com) are both excellent, and I've used them regularly during my travels and research. Lastly, it's worth being aware of the fact that there are often several different spellings for the same word in Spanish.

Understanding
Northern
Spain

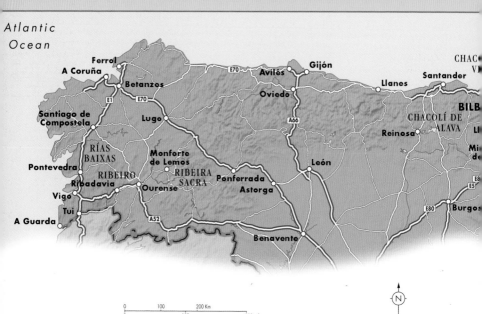

*Atlantic
Ocean*

CHACOLI DE
GUETARIA

Gurnika-
Lumo

FRANCE

SPAIN

Zaráutz
E70

San Sebastián

Vitoria-
Gasteiz

Pamplona

Jaca

ANDORRA

Logroño

NAVARRA

E7

EMPORDA-
COSTA BRAVA

Figueres

L'Escala

LA RIOJA

Huesca

SOMONTANO

Girona

Tudela

COSTERS
DEL SEGRE

A7

E7

Barbastro

E15

E804

ZARAGOZA

Lleida

Sabadell

Mataró

N11

Vilafranca
del Penedès

N11

E90

A2

E90

E90

BARCELONA

Montblanc

PENEDÈS

PRIORAT

Reus

Sitges

MONTSANT

CONCA DE BARBERA

Falset

Tarragona

Mediterranean
Sea

TARRAGONA

Why Northern Spain makes great wines

W hy Northern Spain? Because it has a beautifully varied landscape, because the food is superb, because the people are charming, because you can go canyoning, caving, walking, cycling, and swimming, but most of all because it produces almost every style of wine that it's possible to imagine.

SPANISH WINE FACTS

It isn't possible to separate the figures for the north of Spain, so these facts are for Spain as a whole.

- Spain has **1.12 million ha** of vines dedicated to wine production. This is the largest of any country worldwide and accounts for around **15%** of the **world** total.
- There is an almost exact **50/50 split** between white and red varieties.
- The latest figures from the Spanish Ministry of Agriculture suggest that Spain is the **second largest wine producer** (including grape must) after France, just ahead of Italy. These three countries together account for 54% of total world production.
- **Red** wine accounts for about **50%** of production, white 45%, and the remaining styles 5%.
- Around a third of all Spanish wine is exported and Spain is the **third largest exporter of wine in the world**.
- Wine production (including must) accounts for 2% of total agricultural production.

A journey of surprize and delight

The generally cooler climate enjoyed by the north of Spain means that arguably the finest and most famous wines (with the exception of sherry) are produced here. Each region has its own style, and when you consider the array of indigenous grape varieties, micro-climates, winemaking experience, and technology, there's no wonder such a wide range of wines exists. Alongside chefs, architects, and artists, the winemakers of Northern Spain are more pioneering, innovative, and exciting than ever before.

Galicia and Chacolí, white as snow

Situated in the extreme northwest corner of the country, Galicia is home to some of Spain's finest white wines. The cool, damp Atlantic climate results in a verdant landscape ideally suited to the production of crisp, fresh, mouth-watering whites. Add to this the indigenous Albariño grape, a variety capable of extraordinarily high quality, and you have a recipe for some of the most delicious seafood wines in the world.

Less well known, less exported, and therefore more of a "find", are the wines of the Chacolís, produced around the north-central coast of Spain. Again the Atlantic plays its part, helping to create the ultimate in fish-friendly wines. The interest here lies in the uniqueness of the indigenous Hondarrabi Zuri and Hondarrabi Beltza grapes, varieties which are grown only in the Basque Country.

Shades of red

In Rioja and Navarra, the sea influence is usurped by mountains, undulating sandy slopes, and a warm, dry climate. Unsurprisingly the emphasis here is on red and rosé wines, with the few whites inclining towards a fuller, fleshier form than their coastal cousins.

A fascinating change has started to take place here recently. The situation used to be that Navarra was considered the innovator, whilst Rioja remained the resolute traditionalist with ancient rules governing the production of its wines. Today,

however, you'll find Riojan wine being made in a dazzling array of styles, from staunchly old-school to ultra-modern, whilst Navarra is looking to its historic winemaking roots for inspiration. Navarra also makes some delicious dessert wines.

ABOVE *Rioja's sandy vineyards are traditionally planted to short, squat, en vaso-trained vines.*

Spain's New World
In Somontano every colour of wine is currently being produced, in perhaps the most New World style of any of the northern regions. International varieties are frequently favoured over traditional, and investment in modern technology has been huge.

Cult calling in Priorat and Montsant
The wines of the tiny northeastern region of Priorat are some of the most sought after and expensive in Spain. From a mixture of old-vine Garnacha and Cariñena, sublimely elegant, concentrated, velvet-smooth wines are crafted by pioneering young winemakers with one aim, to make the best red wines in Spain. Neighbouring Montsant provides a good, less expensive alternative.

Fizz and the future in Penedès
Penedès has always been at the forefront of innovation in Spanish winemaking, and if there's one region in Northern Spain where you'll find a wine for every taste, every budget, and every occasion, it's here. Home to Spain's famous sparkling wine, cava, Penedès also produces crisp, fresh whites, elegant full-bodied reds, and boldly fruity rosés, plus sweet wines and brandy.

The people

The story of Spanish wine began over 3,000 years ago when the Phoenicians, who were flogging their wares around the Mediterranean, decided it would be far more sensible to put down roots in Southern Spain and make wine there, than ship it across vast stretches of rough and treacherous open sea.

Middle Easterners

Knowing the legendary sweet tooth of the Middle Eastern nations, it's thought most likely that the vine they brought with them was a variety of Moscatel, which they would have crafted into something suitably sticky and sweet. Conveniently this also meant something less susceptible to spoilage when subjected to heat and poor storage conditions.

BELOW *A traditional tapas bar where Spaniards grab a tasty bite, from tortilla to anchovies or local cheese.*

Italian influence

All that was happening in the south, however, and it wasn't until several more centuries had passed that the Greeks and Phoenicians appeared on the northeastern coast of Spain, around the 6th century BC. The Romans followed close on their heels around 200 BC, and for the next 600 years their rule would spread to most of the country. It is, of course, a well-known fact that the great minds (and bodies) of the Roman Empire were not fuelled by bread alone. They brought with them vines and vineyard techniques, as well as a system of fermentation in open stone troughs which is used to this day – albeit in a very small number of bodegas.

Moor of the same

From the 8th century AD until the middle of the 15th century, things went a little quiet on the wine-making front. The Moors were now in charge and, being good Muslims, they found that distillation was more to their taste and used the process to make their beloved perfumes and aromatic essences. From 1492 and the Christian reconquest of the Iberian peninsula however, wine was finally back to stay.

Modern-day pioneers

Moving into the 19th century, it was France, just a short hike across the Pyrenees, that was to have the biggest influence on Spanish winemaking, and the developments all began in the north of Spain. When the devastating vine louse, phylloxera, threatened to deprive France of its national drink it had no choice but to look to Spain for help. However, although Bordeaux merchants began trading with Rioja and Navarra at this time, it was actually a Spaniard who brought a little French know-how to the vineyards of Rioja.

Don Camilo Hurtado de Amezaga had been booted off to France for penning his political thoughts and, in doing so, seriously upsetting the Spanish authorities. When he returned in the middle of the 19th century he brought with him some Bordeaux casks and an absolute belief that the wines of Bordeaux could be matched, if not bettered, in his homeland. He wasn't exactly welcomed with open arms by his fellow countrymen, and to say they took a bit of persuading to adopt these new Bordeaux techniques is to put it mildly. However, the resulting wines spoke for themselves and if I tell you that he later became Rioja's Marqués de Riscal, you'll know that his success lives on today.

There have been many other hugely important figures in Spain's recent winemaking history – far too numerous to mention here. No one, though, could be considered more influential during the last 40 years than Miguel Torres. He introduced stainless-steel technology into his Catalan winery during the 1960s in a move that was to change the face of modern Spanish wine forever. Fresh, fruity white wines and clean, elegant reds slowly started to alter the reputation of Spanish wine, both at home and abroad.

ABOVE *For non-Spanish speakers, writing postcards may be an easier option than reading* El País.

How it's all mapped out

Today, as a result of the new constitution of 1978, Spain is divided into 17 *autonomías* or autonomous regions, each with its own parliament and a few with their own language. These regions are sub-divided into provinces, of which there are 50.

For the purposes of this book we'll be looking at wine routes in six *autonomías*. They're the ones which span the north of the country from west to east and are: Galicia; the Basque Country; Navarra; La Rioja; Aragón; and Catalonia – each contains one or more wine DO, as well as some designated *vino de la tierra* areas. (You'll find an explanation of these terms on p.25.)

The Basque Country and Catalonia are two of the most powerful *autonomías* in the whole of Spain. The fact that, along with Galicia, they not only have their own government, but also their own language, says something about the wonderful independence of spirit to be found in people right across the north of Spain. The wines produced in each *autonomía* reflect this, being as diverse and individual as the people themselves.

ABOVE *A tile painting from the modernist cooperative in Nulles, Tarragona.*

Slowly does it

If we compare the Spanish to the Australians, however, we begin to see why the revolution in Spanish winemaking hasn't had the same impact on our wine buying practices as the shelves of Chardonnay and Shiraz we were knocked out by in the 1990s. The Aussies hit us full in the face with fruity wines, modern labels, memorable grape varieties, and, above all, a marketing strategy that considered "Brand Australia" to be far more important than the individual wineries and winemakers. It was all so easy to understand, we knew what they were offering us, and we lapped up every last drop of it.

In Spain, although there are a few exceptions, I've seen new winemaking ideas again and again receive the "let's see our neighbours try it first" attitude. They're a proud race with a strong domestic market for wine, so the idea of marketing themselves as one big "united face of Spanish wine" in order to appeal to export markets is almost anathema to them. I have to add that if the majority of wine labels are anything to go by, they don't waste a lot of time studying modern trends in packaging either.

However, the Spanish are some of the most amiable people in the world, and their will to improve and strive for better things is often humbling. "Brand Spain" may never happen, but that's no bad thing, especially when we consider that the young, headstrong pioneers of Northern Spain are currently producing some of the most exciting wines in the world. So the pace may at times seem frustratingly slow and cautious, but only from staunchly individual minds can come unique and extraordinary wines.

Seasons and festivals

As a wine tourist, the best time to visit Northern Spain is spring (April/May) and the end of harvest in October, when you may be offered fresh grape must to taste. During July and August it can be extremely hot and you'll also find that many Spaniards take their own holidays at this time, rendering winery visits impossible and hotel accommodation scarce. Throughout the winter months there will be some work going on in the vineyards, but the vines will be bare, the weather cold, and the landscape not nearly as breathtaking as when it's bathed in golden sunshine.

When to visit

This book covers a large area of land and it's difficult to offer weather predictions that accurately cover all of it. That said, as a general rule, spring and autumn are mild, with warmer temperatures favouring the eastern, Mediterranean corner and the areas further inland, whilst the tempering influence of the Atlantic keeps Galicia and the northern coastline a little cooler.

Bank holidays/día feriado

There are several national, regional, and local public holidays in Spain. On these days most wineries will be closed.

Party time

The Spanish need very little excuse to throw a party or *fiesta*, and it's almost certain that wherever you are in Northern Spain, and at whatever time of year, there'll be some sort of festival taking place close by. If you want to plan your visit to coincide with one of the numerous wine festivals, however, it's a good idea to check out the websites of the local tourist authorities and *consejo reguladors* (detailed in the second part of the book) to see when the next one is being held.

BELOW *Posters for the national sport of bull fighting decorate every street corner of Spain.*

Important wine festivals

Two of the significant annual festivals take place in Rioja. The first is "Fiestas de Haro", held during the last week of June and best known for its famous wine battle, *batalla del vino*, on the small Riscos de Bilibio mountain – and if you're wondering, it's a water fight with wine (www.valvanera.com/fiestasharo.htm).

The second is "Fiestas de la Vendimia Riojana", the Rioja Wine Harvest Festival, which shares its festivities with the "Fiesta de San Mateo" in Logroño for a week around 21 September. The main event is treading the grapes and offering the first must to the Virgen of Valvanera (www.logro-o.org).

In Galicia, the Albariño Wine Fair comes to the coastal town of Cambados on the first Sunday in August. Neighbouring Ribeiro holds its "Feria de Vino del Ribeiro" at the end of April/beginning of May, and in Ribeira Sacra you'll find the "Vino de la Ribeira Sacra" being celebrated in Monforte de Lemos during the last week in May.

The Costers del Segre holds its annual Grape Harvest Festival in the middle of September at Raimat each year (*see* Costers del Segre chapter, p.93). Just next to the cellars there's a grape treading competition, a tasting of the first must, and a show depicting the legend of a plague of rabbits that the area once suffered (www.paeria.es/turisme).

In Priorat, the town of Falset hosts a wine festival during the first weekend of May each year, and in Somontano the DO organizes an artistic festival, held in Barbastro during the first weekend of August – a ticket includes *tapas* and a glass of wine.

Other festivals and events

There are literally hundreds of *fiestas* that you may accidentally, or intentionally, encounter as you travel around – here are three of the most colourful and crazy for you to either target or avoid:

"Fiesta de San Fermín" is held from July 6–14 and is one of the most talked about festivals in Spain. For one week each year the streets of Pamplona throng with people eager to see the bull running and fighting (www.sanfermin.com). For more details *see* Navarra chapter, p.74.

Although nothing to do with Northern Spain, I can't resist the urge to mention the wonderfully ridiculous Tomatina. Held on the last Wednesday in August, it's a two-hour tomato-throwing festival that attracts 30,000 people and involves 125,000 kilos (123 tons) of overripe tomatoes. If it tickles your fancy, head for the Buñol, to the west of Valencia and 400km (250 miles) from Barcelona (www.spain-info.com/culture/tomatofight.htm).

The week-long "Carnaval de Sitges" is held in February each year. It is an extravaganza of colour, costumes, and campery, with the gay community demonstrating their innate ability to throw a fabulous party.

Knowing the wines

Northern Spain is a vast area which boasts one of the most diverse and exciting arrays of wine to be found anywhere in the world. It's an "Old World" country and its winemaking history, which goes back thousands of years, is inextricably linked to the culture and food of the individual regions.

Growing up

The key to understanding the wines of Northern Spain is to look at the region in which a given wine is produced. Consider the climate, the terrain, the proximity to the ocean, and most importantly, the cuisine traditionally enjoyed there.

Let's take Galicia in the west as an example. The landscape is lush and green, the climate cool and damp, and as half of Galicia's border faces the Atlantic Ocean, it's no surprise that seafood reigns supreme. But hungry fishermen are unlikely to be sated by a plate of swordfish *carpaccio* after a hard day at sea and it's more robust fair such as octopus marinated in olive oil, or chunky pan-fried hake, both with a large helping of potatoes on the side, which are most traditionally served. The ideal wine to cut through the richness and yet remain in balance with the flavours is white with good crisp acidity and a reasonable weight of fruit. Albariño is of course absolutely perfect.

Rioja is another example. Further from the sea, the food here tends to be meat based, with *patatas a la riojana* (a hearty dish featuring potatoes and *chorizo*), roasted lamb, spicy sausage and bean stews, and firm, flavourful cheeses all making regular appearances. Because the climate is warmer, red grape varieties are more abundant than white, yet in order to remain food friendly, the wines are rarely heavy or overly alcoholic. Rather they offer everything from bright, juicy red fruits, to spicy vanilla and raisin flavours, with moderate weight. The only exceptions to this are some powerful new *alta expresión* wines.

The same sort of analogy can be applied to almost all the regions of Northern Spain, with the exception of Somontano, whose wines are very much a product of the last 20 years' pioneering work, and are far more heavily influenced by New World wine producers than anything in Aragón's long and varied winemaking history.

LEFT *Seasonal lilacs in bloom at Codorníu in Penedès.*

BELOW *Bottles whiz around the bottling line at Bodegas Bilbaínas in the heart of Rioja.*

So there's usually no great scientific reasoning behind the styles of wine each region produces. It's more to do with history and culture, and a case of farmers having taken what was given to them (or brought in by thirsty invaders) and making the best wine they could from it, always with an eye on a match for their supper. As you travel around, try wines with food as often as you can; that's what they were made for, and that's how they'll taste best.

The grapes

There are literally hundreds of different grape varieties, indigenous and international, grown throughout Northern Spain. In fact, thanks to Catalan winemaking legend Miguel Torres' interest in the rediscovery and propagation of ancient Catalan vines, that area alone boasts well over a hundred different varieties.

The grapes I've chosen to describe below are the most important ones in each region. I've focused on indigenous varieties with just a short paragraph at the end of each section detailing the most cultivated international varieties.

White varieties
Albariño

BELOW *An old wooden wine press is a popular choice for decorating winery gardens.*

Native to the cool, lush green countryside of Galicia, the Albariño grape produces arguably Spain's finest and most exciting white wines. It's certainly the most important grape variety in the Rías Baixas DO where it represents 90% of the vines. The small berries have a high sugar content and the wines are naturally crisp, fresh, and herbaceous, with an attractive, aromatic peachiness.

Many people agree that these wines should be drunk in the flush of youth when all their crisp fruitiness is to the fore. It's therefore surprising to find that 100% malolactic fermentation has traditionally been favoured. Malolactic fermentation is a secondary fermentation used to transform the unripe, green apple character of malic acid into creamier lactic acid, thereby making tight, astringent wines softer and more approachable. It also allows more complex flavours to develop in the wines.

Today attitudes are in a state of flux with producers using anything from 20–100% malolactic in an attempt to find the right balance. What you'll therefore tend to find are two kinds of wine being made, "modern wines" with very low levels of malo and "traditional wines" with 100%. I find that the best wines fall somewhere in the middle. This allows for all the wonderful fruit flavours to express themselves, and for the unique, smoky minerality of good Albariño to be retained. Ask about the percentage of malolactic as you taste various wines and see what you think.

You will find some barrel fermented Albariño being made here and there, but as Ana Quintela of Pazo de Señoráns says, "Oak eats Albariño in a very short time". The wines are more expensive and personally I'd give them a wide berth.

Godello

Again found in the Galician DOs, this is a grape which has really begun to make its mark in recent years. It's believed to be the same variety as the Verdelho grape of Northern Portugal and Madeira (where it's also a wine style). When it's good it has a rich, honeyed orange character, although it is refreshingly dry with lots of juicy acidity. You're most likely to come across it on the Ribeiro and Ribeira Sacra tours of this book.

The big three...

Macabeo (Viura)

Grown all over Northern Spain, this is the first of the three white grape varieties traditionally used to make cava, Spain's most popular sparkling wine. It's a fairly neutral variety which works well as a blending material – in cava it lends crisp, fresh acidity to the mix. As Viura it's also a variety well suited to oak ageing, evidenced in a small amount of stunning white Rioja. In the best of these, the creamy vanilla flavours of the oak coat a dry, tangerine-peel fruit flavoured core to make a luscious yet refreshing wine.

Xarel-lo (Pansà Blanca)

Xarel-lo (pronounced sha-ray-oh), is used to make both cava and varietal still wines, most often in its native Catalonia. It's a vigorous vine which buds early, making it susceptible to spring frosts. It's also prone to oxidation. However, with early picking and careful handling it yields high-quality grapes. In cava it gives structure and power to the blend, whilst as a still wine it's often similar to a full-flavoured, herbaceous Sauvignon Blanc.

Parellada

With its soft, creamy character, this variety adds a "feminine touch" to the cava blend. The grapes are large, as are the bunches, and the vine has a tendency to over-crop if it isn't carefully managed. Like Xarel-lo, it can also produce attractive, easy-going still wines, the most famous of which is arguably Miguel Torres' Viña Sol.

Garnacha Blanca

A relatively low-acid grape used as blending material in north-central to northeastern Spain to soften and plump out wines.

Hondarrabi Zuri

Exclusively grown in the Basque Country, this is a vigorous variety known for its acidity and alcohol, and it makes a beautiful match with the local seafood. It's the main component of the crisp, spritzy Chacolí wines and is especially important in Chacolí de Guetaria.

Malvasia

A grape of Greek origin used to make wines which can be dry,

ABOVE *Part of the extensive barrel cellars at Torres in the Penedès region.*

ABOVE *The old-fashioned way to riddle cava (a process which slowly moves the sediment into the neck of the bottle) was by hand, with the bottles held in specially shaped* pupitres.

sweet, or semi-fortified. There's a small amount in Navarra, and in Rioja (Malvasía Riojana) around 10% is often added to give a bit more structure and ageing potential to the wines.

Moscatel de Grano Menudo

Known as Muscat Blanc à Petits Grains in France, this is the oldest and finest of the various Muscat varieties. Although it's far less widely planted throughout Spain than the inferior Moscatel de Alejandría (Muscat of Alexandria), I've included it because it's the main variety at Bodega Camilo Castilla in Navarra. If there's one wine grape which gives truly "grapey" aromas and tastes, it's Muscat, and at Castilla they squeeze out rich, raisiny liquid – it's like drinking a luscious, boozy Christmas cake.

The internationals

Many areas of Northern Spain are now home to a good deal of Chardonnay, especially Navarra, Somontano, and Penedès. You'll also find some Riesling, Chenin Blanc, Gewurztraminer, and Sauvignon Blanc in the north, as winemakers experiment to improve and expand Spain's white wines. Look out for wines made from these varieties as you travel around and see if you think they taste better, worse, or just different to traditional wines. And where Chardonnay, for example, is blended with an indigenous variety, can you taste it? Does it ultimately make for a better wine?

Red varieties

Tempranillo (Ull de Llebre)

Widely cultivated and highly regarded throughout the whole of Spain, this is the grape which we most readily associate with red Rioja, and more specifically Rioja Alta and Alavesa. Here it grows everywhere on traditional bush-shaped vines. It can be used as a stand-alone varietal, but more usually in Rioja it'll be blended with any or all of the following varieties: Graciano; Mazuelo; Garnacha; and, most recently, Cabernet Sauvignon.

In Spanish, *"temprano"* means early and this is indeed an early ripening grape that can be ready for harvesting up to two weeks before Spain's other popular red, Garnacha. Its flavours are difficult to pin down and can vary according to where the grapes are grown and what the winemaker does with them. However, a mix of fresh and dried red fruits, especially strawberries, raspberries, and dried sour cherries are often present, along with a certain leathery spice and twist of pepper. It can make fresh, early-drinking *jóvenes* wines, but also has the structure to age gracefully, yielding wines with a creamy, raisined spice quality.

Navarra has its fair share of Tempranillo, which it blends to great effect with Cabernet Sauvignon and/or Merlot. Indeed Tempranillo seems to be a new favourite of winemakers the world over, as far afield as Chile, Argentina, California, and Australia – so who knows what the future holds for Spain's noblest red grape?

Garnacha

Popular throughout Northern Spain, Garnacha loves a warm climate and is an important part of the blend in Rioja, where it flourishes in the hotter Baja part of the region. In the typical Riojan blend, Garnacha adds body and approachability.

In Navarra it's perhaps best known for the delicious rosés we associate with the region, and in Penedès, like Monastrell, it makes an appearance as pink cava.

Where it reaches its ultimate expression, however, is in the old-vine wines of Priorat. Here it's usually blended with similarly ancient Cariñena grapes, and some rather more youthful Cabernet Sauvignon, Merlot, or Syrah. The wines it produces are exquisite – rich, ripe, and concentrated with perfumed, dark, creamy fruit, and refreshing acidity.

Graciano

Although grown in tiny quantities, this low-yielding, tough-skinned little variety plays an

BELOW *A benefit of the pergola vine-training system is that the grapes are shielded from the heat of the midsummer sun.*

ABOVE *Vineyard workers help to bring in the harvest in Navarra.*

important role in Rioja. It usually accounts for no more than 10% of the blend, but its colour and especially tannin lend elegance and essential ageability to the wines.

However, the most interesting Gracianos to try are the varietal wines, which can be found at Señorío de Sarría in Navarra and Viña Ijalba in Rioja.

Cariñena (Mazuelo)

The final grape of the Riojan blend is used in small quantities to add colour, tannin, and acidity. As old-vine Cariñena it holds a far loftier position in the Priorat and Montsant DOs of northeast Spain, where it's blended with Garnacha to produce some of Spain's most sought after wines. As with Graciano, you'll also find the odd varietal version being produced, most notably by Marqués de Murrieta in Rioja. In Catalonia it's known as Samsó.

Hondarrabi Beltza

The red partner to the white Hondarrabi Zuri, this variety is similarly found only in the Basque Country's Chacolí region. The two are usually blended together at a ratio of 85% to 15%, with the Beltza lending a smoothness to the spritzy white wine. It's also used to make a small amount of red wine.

Mencía

Mencía is grown in Ribeira Sacra and Ribeiro – in fact, it's the main red variety for all of Spain's northwest corner, being popular in both Galicia and across the border in DO Bierzo. There have been unproved links with Bordeaux's Cabernet Franc. The wines tend to be early drinking with attractive red fruit and soft tannins.

Monastrell

Known as Mourvèdre in France, this is a grape which has excited great interest in Spain's southeast corner recently. It buds late and its small, sweet, thick-skinned berries ripen late. Although down south it's used to produce ripe, heady red wines with dark fruit flavours, in Catalonia it makes frothy pink cava.

The internationals

Cabernet Sauvignon and Merlot are the most popular, especially in Navarra, Somontano, Costers del Segre, and Penedès. Even Rioja has allowed some experimental Cabernet Sauvignon to creep into the blend, adding a sometimes controversial modernity to the wine. A whole host of other red varieties are dotted across the north, although Pinot Noir and Syrah are the most common.

How Northern Spain makes wine

The basic premise behind turning non-alcoholic liquid into wine is the same in Northern Spain as it is the world over. All that's needed is for the water to be sugary, and for it to be fed to some sweet-toothed yeast. These greedy and overindulgent creatures will die a slow but happy death as they steadily gobble up all the sugar and drown in their own wake of alcohol and carbon dioxide fumes.

Each to their own

The bio-chemical reaction described above is more or less the same wherever wine is made, but the important difference is that each individual winery or bodega, in each of the various wine regions of the world, has its own subtle variations on the same theme.

In Northern Spain it depends not only on the style of wine being produced (red, white, sparkling, sweet, oak-aged etc.), but also the amount of money the bodega has at its disposal, and how forward-thinking or traditional its owners are in their approach. It's therefore impossible to say "this is how Northern Spanish wine is made," so as a starting point I'm going to give you a general idea of the stages normally involved in the production of the various styles. Once you know the basics, you'll be able to see who's doing things a little differently and to ask them why.

Red wine

The first step is for the grapes to be harvested. This may be done by hand or by machine, depending on the training of the vines. If, as is often the case in Rioja and Priorat, the vines are grown *en vaso* (like a small, stubby bush), then hand harvesting is the only way. Vines trained on wires can be machine harvested, which is a faster and less expensive option. Once the red grapes have been delivered to the winery they'll be put onto a selection table, where sub-standard bunches will be discarded. The remaining grapes are then de-stemmed and crushed. The de-stemming removes stalks which might impart green, unripe flavours to the grapes, and the crushing allows the colour from the skins to be leached into the wine – all grape juice is initially white, whatever the colour of the grapes.

BELOW *Northern Spain boasts everything from tiny garagiste operations to some of the most technically sophisticated wineries in the world.*

The whole squidgy lot is then put into some sort of vat for fermentation – these can be anything from fibreglass vessels, epoxy-lined concrete tanks, or oak vats, to temperature-controlled stainless steel, or, the most high-tech of all, *autoevacuaciones* (self-emptiers) which work with gravity.

Once the fermentation is complete, the freshly made wine is run off, usually into barrels, and a second malolactic fermentation is often encouraged before the wine is left to age. The purpose of the malolactic fermentation is to force the green apple tartness of the malic acid into creamy, lactic submission, thereby giving the wine a rounder, silkier texture and a more aromatic profile. The solids, which were left behind, are pressed and a small amount of punchy press wine may be used to beef up the final blend. The wine will already have been stabilized and may now undergo filtration before being bottled.

White wine

The obvious difference in white winemaking is that it's not necessary to extract colour from the skins, so the grapes are de-stemmed and immediately pressed when they arrive at the winery. For added flavour and structure, the skins may stay in contact with the juice for a short while, and then fermentation will occur, either in oak barrels or in tanks. The controlled fermentation temperature for white wines is lower than for reds as it's essential not to spoil their delicate aromatic flavours. Red wines also need a slightly warmer fermentation for the skin colour to be effectively extracted. Some white wines undergo a second, malolactic fermentation (*see* above and *Albariño*, p.18), before they're either aged or not, stabilized, blended, and bottled.

Rosé wine

Rosé is made in much the same way as white wine, although from black grapes. The juice stays in contact with the grape skins just long enough for it to achieve the required shade of pink.

Sparkling wine and specialities

Cava is a traditional method sparkling wine and an explanation as to how it's made can be found on p.122.

You'll also taste delicious sweet wines and local specialities as you travel around – these highly individual and fascinating products are dealt with in their appropriate regional chapters.

Tips

Wineries spend a fortune on their bottling lines, and consequently love to show it off at every opportunity. The first one you see in action is utterly fascinating, but believe me, they all do exactly the same job and if you've seen one you've seen them all.

RIGHT *The Oliveda winery in the Empordà-Costa Brava has its own museum of wine taps.*

BELOW *Once the buds burst in spring, it will be approximately 100 days until the vine flowers.*

Ask the winemaker if he or she uses American or French oak, and why. Each imparts its own range of flavours to the wine and it's interesting to learn, and to taste, the difference.

Quality levels
On August 1, 2003, a new national wine law was passed in Spain to update the then current wine law of 1970. Although in the north of Spain it had an immediate effect only on Rioja and cava, over the following years the other DO regions were expected to gradually implement the new law into their own statutes. The number of classified quality levels was increased from four to seven. The new categories appear in bold below.

Table wines
Vino de Mesa; Vino de la Tierra (VdT).

Quality wines
Vino de Calidad con indicación geográfica (VCIG); Denominación de Origen (DO); Denominación de Origen Calificada (DOCa) – currently only Rioja and Priorat.

Exceptional Single Vineyards
Vino de Pago; Vino de Pago Calificado.

Along with these changes to the classification pyramid there have been several other important moves: a new national "Spanish Wine Council" has been set up and charged with creating a central policy for wine; wineries are now permitted to sell wines under their own name from more than one DO (effectively facilitating the creation of "brands"); and a standard system of ageing and age descriptors has been established.

A question of time
It's important to remember that terms such as *crianza*, *reserva*, and *gran reserva* guarantee only that a wine has been aged for a certain period of time before being released for sale and are no official indication of quality. It's more often than not the case, however, that quality-conscious producers will age their wines up to *gran reserva* level only if the structure and breeding of the initial wine are good enough.
Note: *Crianza*, which means "rearing", "breeding", or "maturing",

---

WINERY TERMS

DO *(denominación de origen)*
Official recognition of a quality wine region.

DOCa *(denominación de origen calificada)*
The highest official classification, currently applied only to Rioja and Priorat.

Consejo Regulador
Regulatory body for individual DOs.

Ha (Hectare)
1ha=2.47 acres

barrel *la barrica*
bottle *una botella*
cellar *la cava/la bodega*
grape *la uva*
harvest/vintage *la vendimia*
old *viejo*
tasting *la degustación/la cata*
vine *la vid/la parra*
vineyard *el viñedo*
winery *la bodega una/la adega* (Galician) *un/el celler* (Catalan)

ABOVE *Inside the barrel cellars at Scala Dei winery in Priorat.*

is used as a generic term to describe Spain's ageing regulations, as well as being used to describe a specific wine.

Quality wines

Jóvenes

Fresh, fruity, "young" wines with little or no ageing in wood, usually released in the spring after the vintage.

Crianza

For red wine, a minimum of two years must be spent in the bodega, with six months in oak (the rest of the time is usually spent in bottle). For white or rosé, 18 months must be spent in the bodega, again with six months in oak.

Semi-crianza/Corta-crianza

An unofficial term used when a bodega puts a young wine into oak for a few months but not the full year required for *crianza*.

Reserva

A minimum of three years in the bodega with 12 months in oak for reds, two years with six months in wood for whites and rosés.

Reserva "Especial"

An unofficial tag added to both *reserva* and *gran reserva* wines indicating that better grapes, usually from special vineyard plots, have been used to produce slightly superior wines.

Gran Reserva

For red wines this means a minimum of five years' ageing before the wine is released. At least 18 months of that time is spent in oak and the rest usually in bottle. White *gran reserva* wines are rare and rosés even more so. They must spend four years in the bodega with six months of that time in oak. A superb *gran reserva* white is Marqués de Murrieta's single-vineyard Capellanía (*see* Rioja chapter, Route Three, p.71).

Non DO or declassified DO wines

"*Noble*" indicates the wine has been aged for 18 months in wood and/or bottle. "*Añejo*" is similar to *noble*, but the time is increased to 24 months. "*Viejo*" literally means "old", and these wines have been aged for at least 36 months.

Note: Sparkling wines have their own ageing requirements.

The winemakers

Wineries in Northern Spain fall into two main categories: cooperatives and family-owned estates. A main difference is that co-ops rarely give the focus of attention to the winemaker, while family-run estates hold him, or her, in pride of place.

The cooperatives

There's generally a three-way split with the co-ops: either they're doggedly old-fashioned with no thought of change; old-fashioned but beginning to realize the gains to be made by cleaning up their act and bottling their own wine; or, at best, commercially minded, aiming to make wines for the international market by encouraging growers to produce top-quality grapes, regardless of the quantity.

Family affairs

Whether a small husband and wife operation or one of the biggest winemaking companies in the world, family-owned businesses regard the role of winemaker as a high profile one. It used to be that sons would make wine the same way their fathers had, without questioning quality. During the last 30 years, that way of thinking has changed beyond recognition and wine is now being made by inquisitive young people who've spent time in California, Bordeaux, Chile, and elsewhere, honing their craft and broadening their experience.

Influential winemakers

The north is home to some of the most important, innovative winemakers in Spain. The most influential, both past and present, are: Don Camilo Hurtado de Amezaga, the Marqués de Riscal (Rioja); Enrique Forner (Rioja); Miguel Torres (Penedès); Telmo Rodríguez (Rioja); and Alvaro Palacios (Priorat).

I haven't included any women, but that doesn't mean there aren't some superb female winemakers on the scene – you may, in fact, be surprised by how many you encounter as you travel around.

Tip: You've strolled in the vineyards, smelled the damp stone cellar, seen the bottling line in full swing, and tasted several wines – but have you met the person who actually made the stuff in your glass? Ask who he or she is, how old they are, and where they trained. Showing an interest may lead to an introduction – unless of course it's harvest time.

BELOW *Artisanal, hands-on winemaking at Clos Mogador in Priorat yields "the best wine ever", according to an article in El País newspaper.*

The etiquette of visiting winemakers

The pleasure gained from drinking a bottle of wine bought in a local supermarket can't possibly come close to the feeling it gives you if you've wandered through the vineyards in which the grapes were grown and met the man (or woman) who turned them into wine. In Northern Spain you'll find every sort of winemaking enterprise, from huge corporations to crusty village cooperatives, to tiny little one man bands. At each you'll receive a warm, yet at times quite formal welcome, and although a shirt and tie aren't necessary, looking clean and tidy is the best way to be taken seriously. Here are a few other tips to help your trip run smoothly.

BELOW *This drinking fountain in the central square of sleepy Gratallops (Priorat) shows just how important winemaking is.*

First things first

It's vital that you make an appointment before you visit any winery, whatever its size. The Spanish expect this courtesy, and whether it's a phone call, fax, or email, give plenty of warning that you're coming and an estimated time of arrival. Wineries can often be difficult to find so always ask for directions at the time of booking your visit. Try to carry a mobile phone during the trip so that you can call ahead if you're going to be late or are lost. On that note, it's a good idea to invest time in planning and printing up a realistic itinerary that includes the names and contact details of all the bodegas with which you have appointments.

When you arrive in a new town go straight to the tourist office and ask if they have a map of the local bodegas. A lot of the routes in this book are too long to cover in one day and I've suggested overnight resting spots. However, you still won't manage more than four wineries a day, so don't overbook yourself – it's a holiday after all.

Too busy for tourists

There's an enormous difference between visiting a large winery with its own public relations staff, ready-made tours, video presentations, and purpose-built shop, to calling in on a small husband and wife operation where the wine is made in little more than a garage.

At the former you'll find visits being conducted (in English) all year round and often the best time to visit is September, when the grapes are being harvested and there's a lot to see in both the vineyards and the winery. At the latter, they'll not only be far too busy to deal with any form of visitor during the harvest, they're also likely to be away in July and August, taking a well-earned break before the hard graft begins in earnest.

Remember: you won't be welcome between 1pm and 4pm when most businesses, except restaurants, are closed.

Tongue tied
Northern Spain is a very large area and it's impossible to generalize when it comes to visiting its various wine regions and bodegas. In Rioja, for example, you're almost certain to find that visitors are a regular feature and an English speaking member of the winery staff will be present to meet, greet, and guide you through. In Galicia, on the other hand, you may find that less than half of the wineries are accustomed to visitors and that a few words of Spanish will prove invaluable. I've tried to indicate in each chapter how easy or challenging visits may be.

Playing the professional
In order to be taken seriously by a winemaker, here are a few tips to follow.

Look for something to spit into before you take a sip
Spitting is essential if you're driving, and even if you're not, you won't survive more than two wineries if you don't. In the barrel cellar it's normal to spit into an open drain, in the tasting room you'll need to ask for a spittoon or *"escupidor"*.

Be noisy
Tasting wine properly involves a lot of slurping, sloshing, and sucking, so don't be embarrassed about the noise – it shows that you know what you're doing.

Ask for a price list before you start tasting
You can use it to make notes on the wines – this way you'll appear more interested, and you'd also be amazed how easy it is to forget a wine if you don't make a note.

Ask questions
For example, ask about the grape varieties, the oak ageing, what's permitted and what's not in a given DO. The Spanish are notorious for contradicting each other, so ask the same question at various wineries and take an average of the responses.

Look for the positive
No one likes to hear that the wine they've sweated blood over isn't good. Expressing preferences within a selection is a far more productive option than expressing dislike, and if you simply hate the entire range, then turn the question back on the winemaker and ask what he or she thinks of it.

ABOVE *Codorníu's former press room now houses the company's on-site museum.*

WEBSITES

Some of the winery websites are **under construction** as I write, but I've included their addresses for future reference. The websites which are up and running **vary wildly from being fantastically informative to being utterly useless**. If you find the latter is the case, **forget about emailing** – which is also likely to be a waste of time – and telephone directly instead.

Food and wine culture

In order to understand the Spanish and their attitude to food and wine you need to be familiar with one well-known phrase, "En España se vive en la calle", which means, "In Spain you live in the street". Spain is a Mediterranean country, and even though parts of the north are some of the coolest of its extremities, you still get a sense of life being lived out of doors. You regularly see people bumping into friends, stopping off at a favourite café or bar, indulging in lengthy exchanges of opinion, and watching as their young children play. All the while, local activities are carefully surveyed by the older generation as they take their evening *paseo* or stroll around town. Although this picture applies more often to rural Spain, even in the big cities, where life is lived at a faster pace, the atmosphere is similar.

Time for tapas

It's been said that eating and drinking are a national pastime in Spain – all the more reason to go I'd say. The word *"tapa"* literally means "lid", and although there are various theories as to the origins of *tapas*, the most likely one is that innkeepers in times gone by would cover the top of their customer's drink with a piece of bread to keep out the flies. This led to small snacks being offered and ultimately to the culture of *tapas*, which is arguably one of the most popular styles of eating in the world today.

BELOW *In the tiny fishing village of Guetaria, fresh fish is griddled to perfection in front of your eyes, whilst you sip on a glass of crisp Chacolí wine.*

Tapas (known as *"pinchos"* or *"pintxos"* in much of the north) can be enjoyed as a meal in itself or as an appetizer before supper. Either way it's best to move from bar to bar having a small glass of beer or wine and one *tapa* in each. The speciality of the bar is usually the thing to try. If you ask for a glass of wine you'll probably be given the house wine, which in the case of red is likely to be a fruity *crianza*. It'll be served in a sensibly small measure and will go down beautifully with a plate of *jamón*, *manchego*, or whatever else is on offer.

If you don't want to look like a tourist, remember to boldly throw any used paper napkins straight onto the floor. Keep your cocktail sticks, though, that's how the barman knows what to charge you.

Lazy lunches

The Spanish are traditionally known for taking their main meal in the middle of the day. This involves at least two to three hours of eating, followed by a short siesta, and then back to business at around 4pm. Although this custom is now much less the norm in modern-day Spain, it's worth remembering that most shops, museums, information offices, and anything involving a tour, are likely to be closed between the hours of 1pm and 4pm each day.

ABOVE *Plastic trays of* pimientos de Piquillo *adorn stall after stall at the October market in Puente la Reina.*

Last orders

Unless you have a particular passion for dining alone, you may have to change your eating habits to fit in with Spanish meal times. I remember once trying to book a table for 8pm on a Sunday evening in a tiny rural town. I was met with a flat "No, that's not possible". Thinking that the restaurant obviously didn't open on a Sunday evening, I was about to walk away when the lady I was speaking to explained, "We don't open until nine." I've since found that it's actually far from unusual in Spain to see couples wandering in to eat at 10pm or 11pm in the evening.

Restaurants usually offer a set menu, *"menú del día"*, which can be fantastic value, as the price almost always includes bread, water, and wine. However, this is a wine holiday, and you might want to choose something a little more interesting to drink than the basic *vino de la casa*. In more expensive restaurants it can be a real treat to try the menu *degustación*, which often includes wines chosen to match each dish.

Specialities of the north

There are many "must try" dishes to be found throughout the whole of Spain: *paella, gazpacho, pan con tomate* (see below); *tortilla, patatas a la riojana, calamares,* and *jamón serrano,* to name but a few. And although each northern region has its own unique produce with which to create its signature dishes – from the wonderful seafood of Galicia and the Chacolís, to the local meats and cheeses of the more mountainous inland areas – there are one or two specialities that I'd like to suggest you try:

Pimientos de Padrón – named after a town in Galicia, these come roasted with lots of garlic and salt. Beware, there's always a super-fiery one lurking on the plate.

ABOVE *Rows of sweetcorn drying in the sun decorate many a house in Ribeiro.*

Idiazabal – although it's almost impossible to choose just one product from the Basque Country, famed as it is throughout Spain for the quality of its cuisine, this local sheep's milk cheese is particularly delicious whether eaten raw or cooked.

Crema Catalana – the Spanish are not especially known for their desserts, but this one, which originated in Catalonia, is so famous that it deserves at least a mention. It's a cross between *crème caramel* and *crème brûlée*, but with a baked, rather than a caramelized top.

Pimientos de Piquillo – so important are these red peppers from Navarra that they have their own appellation, "Pimientos Piquillo de Lodosa". If you visit in October, there's a market in Puente la Reina where for two weeks each year you can watch them being roasted to perfection.

Butifarra – a typical Catalan pork sausage which I was served as part of a mixed grill in Lérida. As well as regular *butifarra* there's also "black *butifarra*", which is similar to our own black pudding. Hearty meat dishes are popular here and the rest of my plate was filled with lamb cutlets, grilled rabbit, spicy sausage, roasted red peppers, boiled potatoes, and deep-fried courgettes.

Embuchado – not the most bizarre thing I've ever eaten in Spain, but it's up there. I came across it in La Rioja and foolishly asked what I was eating. Pigs' intestines are wound like wool into something resembling a cricket ball. This is then sliced very thinly and griddled with salt and olive oil. When done properly – whatever you think about eating intestines – the taste is amazing.

Perfect *pan*

If, at the beginning of a meal, your waiter hands you a plate of thickly sliced toast, a couple of whole tomatoes, a few cloves of garlic with their skin on, some salt, and a bottle of olive oil, then it's time to make *pan con tomate*. Begin by rubbing one of the cloves of garlic (unpeeled) vigorously over the surface of the toast. Then, cut a tomato in half horizontally and rub this in the same way, squeezing as you go, over the bread's surface. Next, drizzle liberally with the olive oil and sprinkle with a little salt – and you have the simple but delicious *pan con tomate*.

How to get around

The quickest, cheapest, and easiest way by far to reach the north of Spain is to hop on a plane. The journey time from the UK is less than two hours and even if you're travelling from further afield, with airports conveniently situated across the whole of the north, there shouldn't be any problem finding somewhere suitable to fly into.

By air

There are three major airports serving Northern Spain's wine regions: Barcelona, Bilbao, and Santiago de Compostela. The last part of the journey which carries you from Northern Europe over the Pyrenees and into Spain is breathtaking on a sunlit summer's evening. The airport at Bilbao was designed by Santiago Calatrava, the same architect who designed the Ysios winery in Rioja, and as you descend it appears like a majestic white bird out of the rugged green landscape.

Thanks to low-cost airlines, it's now possible to fly from the UK to Spain for less than it costs to buy a return train ticket from London to York. Easyjet (www.easyjet.com) flies to Bilbao and Barcelona, and Ryanair (www.ryanair.com) to Santiago de Compostela. Both airlines also offer flights to some of the smaller Northern Spanish airports such as Reus, Santander, Girona, and Oviedo.

If you're not too concerned about price and would prefer a service with more suitable flight times or the option to upgrade to a higher class of ticket, then BA (www.ba.com) and Iberia co-chair flights to all three of the major airports mentioned above, although the flight to Santiago de Compostela goes via Madrid.

By train

Once you've landed you may prefer to catch a train to your chosen wine region, thereby allowing yourself some time to relax and enjoy the Spanish countryside before you pick up a car and head off into the heart of the wine country. www.renfe.es has information about all the national and regional train routes, including timetables and prices.

USEFUL WORDS

centro town centre
todas direcciones all directions
autopista motorway
salida motorway exit
dirección unica one-way street
peligro danger
despacio slow
prohibido el paso no entry
obras roadworks
ruta nacional (RN) non-motorway highway

BELOW *Some of the most breathtaking scenery in the whole of Northern Spain is to be encountered on the drive from Leyre to Huesca.*

TIPS FOR DRIVING

- Carry a **bottle of water**.
- **Check your change** at toll booths.
- **Fill up your hire car with petrol** before you return it to Barcelona airport. There's no petrol station and you'll be charged an exorbitant fee if it's empty.
- Watch the **speed limits**: motorway 120km/hr (74.5 miles/hr); major roads 90–100km/hr (56–62 miles/hr); towns 50km/hr (31 miles/hr); residential areas just 20km/hr (12.4 miles/hr).
- **Never drink and drive.** The Spanish take this very seriously and if you have more than 0.25mg of alcohol per litre of blood (in the UK it's 0.4mg) in your system, you could face jail.

BELOW *Taking toll motorways is far faster and quieter than the heavily used national roads.*

Public transport and cycling

Although public transport is an option in some areas, the limitations of the service will make any true journey of discovery virtually impossible. Hiring bicycles is another way of getting from one winery to another, and of working off all that lovely food and wine as you go. Contact the local tourist offices for more information.

By car

By far the best way of travelling the routes described in this book is by car. You may even choose to maximize any potential wine buying by driving to Spain in your own vehicle, although do remember that if you're visiting in summer, wine will deteriorate rapidly if it's made to sit in a hot boot for days on end.

For reasonably priced car hire try www.holidayautos.co.uk or www.carhireexpress.co.uk (which also operates a service for visitors from the USA, Canada, and the rest of Europe). Cars can be hired at all major airports and most major towns. At the time of writing, to hire a small car with air conditioning (essential if you're visiting in summer) for one week in September costs around £130.

Via Michelin

I've not only used the superb Michelin road map (£11.99 from most good bookshops) during all of my travels around Northern Spain, I've also used the website www.viamichelin.com, which estimates the distance, toll and petrol charges, and time of any journey. Bear in mind that road numbers may vary if you're using a different map.

Note: You will get lost, everybody does, especially in the larger towns where road signs can be infuriatingly ambiguous. Just try to stay calm and remember that each wrong turn may lead to an unexpected new bodega.

Tolls

All "A" roads are toll roads, and using them can add a substantial amount to your travel expenses if you're going to be staying for any length of time, and doing a reasonable amount of driving. www.autopistas.com will give you more information on prices and methods of payment. However, it's worth mentioning that for this very reason motorways are far less congested and much faster than other major roads.

Where to stay

W herever you travel in Northern Spain you'll find somewhere comfortable and clean to stay. At times, in rural places, the only accommodation comes in the form of a modest *pensión*, whilst other villages boast beautifully converted old farmhouses, and in the larger towns you'll find an extensive choice of hotels and other options available. If you're planning a trip of any length I'd recommend you stay in at least a couple of different types of establishment, both for variety and for the experience.

What to book

When booking a double room in Spain, beware of asking for a "*doble*", however logical it may seem. What you'll invariably end up with is a twin-bedded room, and only if you request a "*cama de matrimonio*" can you guarantee to be given a double bed.

Always check if breakfast is included in the price; it rarely is and can cost anything from 3 euros each. In the most basic *pensións* you'll be served a simple continental breakfast of orange juice, tea or coffee, and crusty bread with butter and jam. If you're asked what you'd like, then be prepared to pay more if you choose fresh fruit and yoghurt. In the larger hotels and state-run *paradores* an extensive buffet breakfast, complete with wine or cava, is usually the norm.

Rural tourism

Most regional websites that you'll come across will have links to local accommodation options, which frequently include rural farmhouses and small family-run guest houses. A good website to look at for environmentally friendly rural accommodation is www.ecoturismorural.com, although it is a little difficult to negotiate this site if you don't speak Spanish.

Throughout the routes in this book I've included as many websites belonging to accommodation associations as possible. Often they'll have a rural bias, as I for one am convinced that staying in small out-of-the-way locations is actually the best way to discover what Spain is really all about.

Consider dinner

Sometimes in the smaller wine regions, the loveliest hotels and guest houses are situated in the middle of the countryside, a good distance from the main local

BELOW *Castillo el Collada in Laguardia is one of Rioja's most charming hotels – and just a stone's throw away from the stunning Ysios winery.*

ABOVE *Hotel Passamaner is a romantic hideaway just above Reus with full spa facilities and two "royal" suites, complete with their own private pools.*

town. If you choose to stay in such a place do remember that your dining options will be reduced to one, your hotel. That is unless you're prepared to drive into town and abstain from alcohol during dinner – which is somehow unlikely on a wine holiday.

The solution: if you're taking a week's holiday in Priorat, for example, plan to spend three nights in Falset (where you can try out all the good restaurants), a couple of nights at a *hostal* in Gratallops (where rural Spain really comes into its own), and a couple of nights in Hostal Antic Priorat with its elegant rooms, stunning views, and honest home cooking (*see* p.111).

Campsites

Spain has hundreds of campsites, many located near coastal resorts and other popular holiday destinations. Whereas in France and Italy sites have an official star rating, in Spain they're ranked by category from first to third – an indication only of the ratio of facilities to pitches. www.vayacamping.net is a useful and easy to navigate site. An annual *Guía de Campings* is also published.

Hotels

The excellent government-run chain of *"parador"* hotels (www. parador.es) was established in the 1920s during the regime of dictator Primo de Rivera. Most are housed in beautiful historic buildings such as medieval castles, former monasteries, ancestral mansions, and old palaces, although those which have been newly constructed can be equally impressive. I've stayed in some of the 86 hotels and although I'd normally advocate seeking out a hidden rural retreat, you'd be missing a wonderfully Spanish experience if you didn't spend at least one night in a *parador*.

Prices range from 75–245 euros for a double room, with breakfast at 11–15 euros per person. *Parador* restaurants are well-known for the quality of their traditional regional cuisine, though you will pay a premium for eating in such splendid surroundings.

Another smart chain is AC Hotels (www.ac-hotels.com), while www.innsofspain.com offers over 150 small hotels and inns which, like the *paradores*, are often converted monasteries and castles, and are usually independently owned.

There is a fashion in Spain for renovating old hotels with an ultra-trendy, minimalist interior design format – usually including a good deal of dark wood, chrome, bold colours, animal-skin prints, and cube-shaped furniture. Though not to everyone's taste, it's remarkable how inexpensive such stylish accommodation can be – so take the opportunity if this type of design appeals.

STAYING AT A WINERY

Wherever possible **I've indicated the wineries which currently have guest rooms or run a small hotel,** but things are changing all the time and **it's always worth enquiring about accommodation** when you make an appointment to visit. If a winery doesn't have its own rooms, the owners will often be able to suggest somewhere that they know of locally, and in my experience these are **some of the best recommendations** you'll be given.

Time out from wine

When you simply can't face any more sniffing, swirling, sipping, and spitting, it's time to head off and sample some of Northern Spain's other delights, and there's no end of possibilities. Whether its monasteries, markets, art, or eating that most appeal, you're bound to find something to suit your wined-out mood.

The markets

If there's any space in your luggage after you've squeezed in as many bottles as possible, Northern Spain has some wonderful food markets where you can stock up on all manner of culinary delicacies. La Boqueria on Barcelona's famous "Ramblas" is unbeatable and, even if you can't fit another thing into your suitcase, just to wander around and gaze at endless stalls teeming with giant, glassy-eyed fish and brightly coloured fresh vegetables is a treat in itself. If you're in need of sustenance there are several stand-up snack bars and a good lunch restaurant at the back of the market.

Logroño, Reus, and Pamplona too have superb central markets where you'll get at least three times as much *chorizo*, *serrano*, or *manchego* for your money as you would at home. Many stalls are able to vacuum pack meat to order, so getting it home in an edible state is no problem at all.

The two big "B"s with two big "G"s

Spain has always been associated with a hugely vibrant art scene, and world-famous works by artists such as Picasso, Miró, Dalí, and El Greco can be seen in galleries the country over. To fly into Barcelona and not take the time to experience one of Antoni Gaudí's extraordinary creations, however, would be to miss some of the most unique and influential art that Spain has ever known. My personal

BELOW *The Salvador Dalí Museum in Figueres is as bizarre as you'd expect it to be.*

ABOVE *Most restaurants in small villages such as Gratallops open only for lunch and Saturday evening dinner.*

WALK THE PILGRIMS' ROUTE

This isn't really a serious suggestion, but **after sampling the delights of this beautiful land you may just feel moved to return and cross it on foot**, perhaps even turning your journey into a **"wine pilgrimage"**. Travelling through Northern Spain in this way would have its benefits of course – there'd be no need to worry about drink driving, the daily trek would effectively dispel any hangover you may be suffering from, and, most importantly, **you'd get to taste just about every style of wine imaginable**. There are several guidebooks on the Pilgrims' Route to Santiago, **the "Camino"**, if the idea happens to appeal.

---

favourite, though by no means the most famous, is *La Pedrera* (on Passeig de Gràcia 92). Bilbao found fame more recently when it became home to architect Frank Gehry's Guggenheim museum. The exterior of the building is astonishing, and inside you'll find a space filled with Gehry's beloved light, curves, and calm (www.guggenheim-bilbao.es).

Go to the beach

It was Spain's beautifully unspoilt northeastern coastline which first attracted sun-seeking tourists back in the 1950s, and although today the word "unspoilt" isn't quite as appropriate, there are still plenty of lovely beaches to discover all the way from Cambrils in the south to the northern border with France. If you prefer a less glamorous and somewhat cooler location, the beaches that fringe north-central Spain, to the east of Bilbao, or those over to the west on Galicia's Atlantic coastline will be more to your taste.

El Montserrat

Northern Spain boasts more than its fair share of monasteries and ancient religious buildings, with the cathedral in Santiago de Compostela being considered the most strikingly beautiful and the most visited by tourists and pilgrims alike. The next most popular destination for pilgrims is Catalonia's Monastery of Montserrat, with its famous Black Virgin, "La Moreneta". Tucked into the side of the dramatic Mountain of Montserrat – the name means "serrated" and refers to the shape of the gnarled, old, weather-worn rock formations – the monastery, with its virgin and famous Basilica boys' choir, is just an hour's train and cable car ride from Barcelona. (*See* www.barcelona-tourist-guide.com/montserrat-spain.html for information on the history and www.fgc.net for how to get there by the FCG train.)

Echaurren

Throughout the following chapters of this book I've suggested some of my favourite eateries, from the simplest of *tapas* bars to top Michelin-starred restaurants. If you drive 30 minutes southwest of Rioja, however, you'll find a restaurant like no other. At Echaurren in Ezcaray (tel: +34 941 354 047; www.echaurren.com), a mother and son cook in the same kitchen and yet have their own adjoining restaurants. Marisa Sánchez favours traditional Riojan cuisine (her chick-pea potage with monkfish and clams is legendary), whilst her son, Francis Paniego, is of the modern school of Spanish cooking and spends his days conjuring up such dishes as lamb's tongue on mango with foie gras, coffee couscous, and Coca-Cola reduction. I guarantee you'll know immediately which "side" you're on, and if you need help with choosing a wine, Marisa's second son and sommelier, José Felix, is always on hand to help.

How to get your wine home

As you travel around you'll taste some delicious wines and the urge to buy will be strong. After all, you're on holiday, you're feeling relaxed, and you're listening to a winemaker who's passionately bringing the wines to life for you. Add to that the attractive price tags and the temptation is irresistible.

By car

To avoid finding yourself with six cases of wine to squeeze into your suitcase, it's best to make a few decisions before you set off. If you've driven from the UK, then there's very little stopping you buying almost as much wine as you like. Within the EU it's relatively easy to transport wine, as long as it's for your own consumption or personal gifts, and not intended for re-sale.

Her Majesty's Revenue & Customs (www.hmrc.gov.uk) allow you to bring 90 litres (10 cases) of wine into the UK. If you get caught with more, without a good reason, then at best your goods may be confiscated, and at worst you could be sent to prison for seven years.

If you're travelling around the region in a hire car the issue of transporting wine becomes more tricky. The easiest option is to set yourself a limit at the beginning of the holiday and, if there are two of you, restrict your buying to no more than 12 bottles, which you can carry home between you. Tip: Be very careful to pad and pack your wine tightly if you're putting it in a suitcase.

Note: If you're visiting in the summer, take your wine into your hotel room each night to avoid it spoiling in the heat of the sun.

Posting

Restrictions apply on posting wine to certain countries, such as the USA. Also, wineries are unlikely to have suitable padded cartons for posting, so you'll need to source those yourself. When you consider the hassle and the cost of postage, unless the wine is very expensive or unavailable outside Spain, it would frankly be better to buy it directly from the UK importer.

Occasional importer

To find out about becoming an occasional importer, contact HMCE (*see* above). This is useful if you find a producer you particularly like and want to buy their wines on an infrequent basis. You'll need to employ a carrier, so be prepared to pay both their charges and the duty on the wine (currently £1.22 and £1.65 per bottle of still and sparkling wine respectively), as well as the ex-cellar price.

BELOW *You'll need to sniff out a local wine shop to buy wine from small cellars that are closed to the public. Prices are similar to those at the winery.*

Discovering Vineyards in Northern Spain

Galicia

I f you've never been to Spain's extreme northwest corner, you could be forgiven for thinking that your plane had taken a wrong turn and dropped you off in Ireland or Wales instead. As you step outside the airport at Santiago de Compostela you're likely to be greeted by cool, damp mists and lush, green countryside, a world apart from the dry, arid landscapes and warm Mediterranean sunshine you might expect further south.

Sea green

Sitting as it does atop Portugal and bordered on all other sides by mountains and ocean, Galicia is physically set apart from the rest of Spain and is considered the poor relation, lagging behind in an increasingly technological and business-oriented world. The region has its own language, "Gallego" (related to Portuguese), as well as strong Celtic traditions which pre-date Christianity. I remember each year, on our family holiday to Wales, being bought a plastic doll dressed in traditional bonnet and apron, and you'll find similar such souvenirs as you amble through the streets of Santiago de Compostela, where the melancholy strains of the local *gaiteros* (Galician bagpipe players) drift enchantingly through the air.

Wine country

Galicia is an *autonomía* which is sub-divided into the four provinces of A Coruña, Ourense, Pontevedra, and Lugo. It has just over 28,000ha under vine and its wines come from five individual DO areas. Three of these appear in this book (heading inland): Rías Baixas, Ribeiro, and Ribeira Sacra.

Thanks to its climate and Atlantic-influenced cuisine, Galicia produces mostly white wines, made from varieties that you're unlikely to encounter elsewhere in Spain: Albariño; Godello; Treixadura; Caiño Blanco; Loureira; Torrontés; and Palomino (an inferior grape that's now in decline). It's the same story for the small amount

BELOW *Mist hanging over pergola-trained vines is a familiar sight in Galicia.*

of red wine produced here from the little-known Mencía, Caiño, and Ferrón grape varieties.

Pilgrims' Route

Since the 9th century pilgrims have faithfully tramped *El Camino de Santiago* (the Pilgrims' Route) across the north of Spain to Galicia's medieval capital, Santiago de Compostela – and I've a sneaky feeling that a great deal fewer would have made it, were it not for the rejuvenating effects of the *vino tinto* they encountered along the way. But the question is why? What single person or objective could inspire such long and arduous journeying, however beautiful the scenery or intoxicating the wine?

The answer is Santo Iago (St James, Spain's patron saint), whose remains are said to lie hidden beneath the high altar of the cathedral, and it's to his tomb that pilgrims come to pay homage, in the hope that their allotted time in purgatory may be thereby lessened. St James was one of Christ's apostles who came to Spain to spread the gospel after the crucifixion. He subsequently left and, after he died, his body was returned to Galicia on a magical unmanned boat. He was then buried and, it seems, forgotten about for 750 years, until his body was rediscovered. As legend has it, he then appeared on the battlefield where courageous Christian soldiers were fending off the Moors. The cathedral is said to be built over the very spot where his bones were found back in 813.

Fishy feast

Fish and seafood grace every table in Galicia and local specialities include scallops, large prawns, barnacles, baby eels, oysters, mussels, lamprey, spider crab, hake, and, most ubiquitous of all, *pulpo* (octopus), which is served warm and meltingly tender with potatoes, paprika, and olive oil. Note: www.turgalicia.es is a useful website for checking restaurant and hotel information.

Wine fiestas

The Spanish love any excuse for a party, and nowhere is this truer than in Galicia. When it comes to wine there's an Albariño festival in Cambados, Ribeiro holds the Feria de Vino del Ribeiro, and Ribeira Sacra the Vino de la Ribeira Sacra in Monforte de Lemos. *See* p.16 for details of when each takes place.

A FEW THINGS YOU MAY NOT KNOW ABOUT GALICIA

• You'll see the words *adega* and *pazo* on wine labels. The first is Galician for *bodega* and the second for a country house or *villa*.
• The scallop shell is the symbol of St James and you'll see it in shops and on buildings everywhere.
• General Francisco Franco was born here in 1892.
• The local cheese is called "*tetilla*" (nipple) because of its shape.
• Estrella beer is brewed in A Coruña.
• Galicia has 750 beaches.
• Amancio Ortega began his career working for a shirtmaker in A Coruña – he now owns the fashion chain Zara and is allegedly Spain's richest man.

Rías Baixas

Beginning at a point to the west of Santiago de Compostela and stretching down to the border with Portugal, the Rías Baixas are the four lower estuaries of Galicia's southwest corner. It's no surprise to find that many Spaniards choose to spend their holidays relaxing on the numerous little beaches and coves that pepper the coastline here. If you too love sea air, seafood, good wine, and stunning architecture, there's no better place to be.

The DO and its zones

Rías Baixas was officially granted DO status in 1988 and its wine areas fall into five separate sub-zones within the province of Pontevedra. The largest and newest of these is Ribeira do Ulla which was created in 2000 and covers an area to the southeast of Santiago that lies around the town and east of A Estrada. The second most recent zone to be recognized (in 1996) is Soutomaior, a tiny area to the southeast of Pontevedra.

However, we're going to be travelling around the other three zones, and the first of these is Val do Salnés. This is the original sub-zone and, thanks to its situation around the coastal town of Cambados, it's the coolest and wettest. Although it's not physically the largest zone, it does have the most area under vine and it's reputed to produce the best wines in the region. The second, O Rosal, begins on the coast around A Guarda and runs into the third, Condado do Tea, as they track the course of the Río Miño inland along the border with Portugal.

White wines and Albariño

Back in the 1950s, people made wine in Rías Baixas purely for home consumption and until 20 years ago nobody outside the region really gave the wines a second thought. However, with the creation of the DO and the subsequent advances that took place in the early 1990s, winemaking here has improved beyond recognition and today these wines are some of the most sought after in Spain.

This is white wine country and over 90% of the vineyard area is planted to Albariño, a grape variety of superb quality that grows in tightly packed bunches and yields deeply coloured grapes that are capable of producing world-class wines. For more on Albariño, see p.18 "Knowing the wines".

LEFT *The magnificent cathedral of Santiago de Compostela is the final stop for the thousands of pilgrims who cross Northern Spain each year.*

BELOW *The cruceiro (religious stone cross) dates back to the 14th century and can symbolize a vow, stand as a memorial, or simply mark a particular road.*

USEFUL INFORMATION
. . . .
**Turismo Santiago
de Compostela**
Rúa do Vilar 43
Tel: +34 981 584 081
www.santiagoturismo.com
**www.doriasbaixas.com
www.riasbaixas.org
www.riasbaixas.com
www.turgalicia.es**

BELOW *Crisp, zesty
Albariño wine is the
perfect accompaniment to
Galicia's abundant seafood.*

Most vines are terraced and planted on pergolas supported by granite posts. This allows for good airflow around and through the grapes, keeping them free from the dangers of rot in what is a very humid climate. Also, in a poor area such as this where land is expensive and holdings often tiny, it was traditionally essential that farmers could grow additional crops beneath the vines. Winemaking here is small-scale and labour intensive, with most of the grapes harvested by hand. For this reason the wines will never be cheap – when was the last time, for example, that you saw discounted Albariño? But quality is generally high and the best wines are worth every penny.

In Val do Salnés, the DO regulations state that wines must be at least 70% Albariño. The style is zesty and fresh with crisp acidity, lemon/apricot fruit, and dried herb minerality. In O Rosal the blend must include a minimum of 70% Albariño and Loureira, and in Condado do Tea there must be 70% Albariño and Treixadura. In practice, a great deal of 100% Albariño is made, with the wines produced further south showing spicy, tropical notes due to the warmer climate.

Getting there
You'll be flying into Santiago de Compostela when visiting Galicia, and from there regular trains run to Pontevedra (around one hour) and Vigo (around 1.5 hours). In order to get around the routes, though, a car is necessary.

Travelling around
Route One summary This route starts in Vilariño, just east of Cambados (around 64km/40 miles southwest of Santiago de Compostela), and from here heads to the coastal town of Cambados, then east to Ribadumia, before continuing northeast through Leiro and Lois to the tiny village of Vilanoviña. The route is approximately 24km (15 miles).
Route Two summary Beginning on the border with Portugal at Tui, this route heads southwest on the C550 into O

Route One: Val do Salnés
24km (15 miles)

Route Two: O Rosal
76.5km (47.5 miles)

Route Three: Condado do Tea
76km (47.2 miles)

N

Condado do Tea

O Rosal

Ribeira do Ulla

Soutomaior

Val do Salnés

SANTIAGO DE COMPOSTELA

A Ramallosa
Luou
Susana
Vedra
N550
Pontevea
A9
Padrón
Barcala (Sta Mariña)
Paradela
Baloira
N640
A ESTRADA
Foxo
Ponte Valga
Nigoi
Catoira
C550
Cuntis
Codeseda
VILAGARCÍA DE AROUSA
Focarei
Vilanova de Arousa
N640
Caldas de Reis
Vilanoviña
N550
Lois
Campo Lameiro
N541
Folgoso
Vilariño
A Ermida
Cambados
Leiro
San Antoniño (Barro)
Sacos
Ribadumia
Barrantes
Caroi
Bearíz
O Grove
C550
Lérez
A Chán (Cotobade)
Armenteira
E
Meaño
PONTEVEDRA
Aguasantas
Seixido
Amiudal
Sanxenxo
Ponte Caldelas
A Lama
Embalse de Alborellos
MARÍN
C531
Berducido
Caseiro
Figueirido
Rial (Soutomaior)
Cabo Udra
Bueu
C550
Amoedo
Ribadavia
A52
A9
C531
Piñeiro
Aldán
Moaña
REDONDELA
Cangas
Cepeda
Illas Cíes
VIGO
Lavadores
Covelo
Filgueira
N120
Ría de Vigo
Mos
Prado
Mondariz
A Cañiza
Lamosa
C550
Beade
N120
PONTEAREAS
A52
Cabo Silleiro
Nigrán
A9
Porriño
Crecente
Vincios
Fornelos
Baiona
Gondomar
Salceda de Caselas
O Castelo (Salvaterra de Miño)
Arbo
Area
As Neves
Tebra
N550
Caldelas
Arantei
Tui
Areas
Arrabal (Oia)
O Seixo
PORTUGAL
C550
Fornelos
Goián
O Rosal
San Juan de Tabagón
A GUARDA
San Miguel de Tabagón
Miño

0   5   10 Km
0   5   10 miles

Rosal and then continues into the coastal town of A Guarda, before heading north and inland to Fornelos, then back out to Oia, and then up the coastal road to Baiona. This route is 76.5km (47.5 miles) long.

Route Three summary

Again this route starts in Tui on the border with Portugal, but heads east following the Río Miño to Porto (near Caldelas), Arantel, and Arbo, before continuing to Ribadavia for the night. This route is 76km (47.2 miles).

Route One: Val do Salnés

Spending a night in the region's medieval capital, Santiago de Compostela, allows you to visit the cathedral, buy some of the local *tetilla* cheese from La Casa de Los Quesos Artesanos on Cantón do Toural, and drink a rich, creamy hot chocolate at Café Santiagués. You could also stay in the flagship five-star *parador*, Hostal dos Reis Católicos (tel: +34 981 582 200; www.santiago@parador.es), and eat some of the region's finest food at Toñi Vicente on Rosalía de Castro 34. Any guidebook on Spain will have lots of information about the city and its history, or just ask at the local tourist office when you get there.

The feminine touch

On this route you'll visit four of Val do Salnés' top bodegas, and in three out of these four you'll find a female winemaker. I have my own theory about this, which has absolutely no scientific reasoning behind it, just feminine intuition. Albariño is a wine which must be made with a feather-light touch. The grapes need swift and delicate handling from the moment they're picked to the time of bottling, in order to preserve all their deliciously fresh, fruity aromas and flavours. Once bottled, Albariño gives immediate pleasure, and although you can wait whilst it ages and develops to elegant, steely maturity, you don't have to. Now I'm not in any way suggesting that all male winemakers practise their craft like a bull in a china shop and make wines to be enjoyed only after they're dead and buried, far from it, it's just that women appear to understand the fragile and capricious needs of Albariño extremely well.

As big as it gets

Martín Códax is situated in Vilariño just off the PO300 as you head inland from Cambados. This is the largest wine company in Rías Baixas and, at around two million bottles a year, it's producing 10% of the region's total. The company was created in 1986 as a cooperative, for very practical reasons. Galicia's ancient laws of inheritance had led to people owning minuscule plots of land which they clung onto for dear life, partly because of their value in such a popular tourist destination, and partly because traditional pride wouldn't allow the disgrace of selling your inheritance. This meant that it was almost impossible to establish an estate of any size, so Martín Códax was born of a need to pool the resources of several local farmers.

This happened at a time when Spain was returning to democracy after the dictatorship of General Franco, a time when the natural artistic nature of the Galician character was free to express itself once more. When a name was needed for the winery and its wines, the company looked to the region's ancient musical traditions and chose the most famous of Galician troubadours, Martín Códax, as their champion.

The company currently produces four Albariño wines, all of which can be tasted on an hour's guided tour of the winery.

Don't forget before you enter the winery to look behind you and out to sea at the rafts collecting mussels, scallops, and oysters — you may find yourself eating them for supper.

A walled vineyard

From Martín Códax drive back into the coastal town of Cambados where you'll find an old 2ha vineyard and the bodega of Palacio de Fefiñanes,

LEFT *Martín Códax offers spectacular views out across the Ria de Arousa, one of Galicia's Rías Baixas or "low estuaries".*

BELOW *The walled vineyard of Palacio de Fefiñanes sits in the middle of Cambados town.*

ABOVE *Don't expect the typical Spanish sunshine and clear blue skies in Rías Baixas. The weather here can be damp and misty.*

tucked behind Praza de Fefiñanes. The vineyard is not only very pretty with its pergola-trained vines and scarlet roses, it's also worth seeking out as it's virtually unique to find a vineyard in the middle of a town. Winemaker Christina Montilla makes one of the best Albariños in the region, Albariño de Fefiñanes, which can be bought here in the shop for a mere 7 euros. There's also an oaked wine and a special blend called 111 Año, but they're both more expensive and frankly less exciting.

For a completely traditional seafood lunch, Ribadomar, with its pretty, pink, flower-bedecked windows and old Spanish couples tucking into huge platters of assorted shellfish, is perfect. Here, as well as *pulpo* (octopus), *merluza* (hake), *lubina* (sea-bass), and every sort of shellfish you can imagine, you'll find a superb selection of local Albariño wines at very reasonable prices.

An Englishman abroad

Galicia is still quite a rural place and if you don't speak Spanish then getting around, using websites, arranging visits, and even ordering the right food can be challenging at best. So when the fun of it all has momentarily worn off, I'd suggest you drop in on Bodegas Castro Martin, where you'll find the most down to earth and friendly of English welcomes awaiting you. Andrew McCarthy's story is the stuff of fairytales and as such it definitely merits a mention. He first visited Rías Baixas as an English wine buyer in 2001 and came to Castro Martin in search of top-quality Albariño wine to sell in the UK. As it turns out he got more than he bargained for, because he found not only the wine he was looking for but also a wife in the form of the delightful Angela Martin, winemaker and daughter of the bodega's founder.

In 2002 they introduced a superior wine, Castro Martin, to the range. The new wine is made entirely from grapes grown in the bodega's own vineyards and is wonderfully elegant with a rich lemon meringue pie nose and juicy lemon concentration on the palate.

Bodegas Castro Martin is in Ribadumia and you'll need to head back out of Cambados on the PO300 before turning right just after Vilariño. Bodegas are not always easy to find in this area, so if in doubt just give Andrew a quick call to check the route.

Three – or four – times a lady

From Castro Martin take the PO9305 for 5km (3 miles), turn right onto the PO9504 for a further 3km (2 miles), turn right onto the PO300 and almost immediately left onto the PO9508 for 3.5km (2.2 miles). Finally turn left onto the PO531 for just under a kilometre (a third of a mile) which should bring you to Vilanoviña and Pazo de Señoráns. Here you'll find the third and final female winemaker on this route, Ana Quintela, as well as her boss and the "grande dame" of the DO, María Soledad Buena. The estate was bought in 1979 by María Soledad and her husband. A former biologist with no experience of winemaking, María Soledad took on the running of the estate and planted the land with kiwis and Albariño grapes. She's a formidable lady with a deep husky voice and a manner that suggests she expects to be listened to. This quality has no doubt proved invaluable since her election to president of the *consejo regulador* in 1986. At the time, having a grape variety as the name of the DO (it was then DO Albariño) led to enormous complications, and it was she who pushed for the change in 1988 to "DO Rías Baixas".

She also turned her hand to winemaking in 1989 and today the bodega produces two wines, one of which is particularly special as it's made from selected old vines and spends 38 months on its lees in small tanks. It's a deliciously rich and spicy, deeply coloured wine, with melon, mandarin, orange, and quince flavours. You won't see it in the UK, so if you like it, buy a couple of bottles while you can.

Route Two: O Rosal
Route Three: Condado do Tea
These are two simple routes which head west and east of Tui respectively, along the border with Portugal.

Tui to A Guarda
Tui is an attractive medieval town with an imposing cathedral and a pleasant little old town where you'll find plenty of good restaurants. It sits on the banks of the Río Miño and if you fancy ambling over the river into Portugal from here, you can do so via the old iron bridge.

Route Two heads west out of Tui towards A Guarda along the C550. Around the towns of San Juan and San Miguel de Tabagón you'll find a couple of good wineries within a stone's throw of each other: Terras Gauda and Santiago Ruiz.

Chunky wines
O Rosal is further south than Val do Salnés, and the wines here start to show fuller, spicier, and often waxier flavours and textures in the mouth. The flagship wine is Terras Gauda, which is a blend of 70% Albariño with Loureira and Caiño Blanco and is a good example of the chunkier style. At the tiny bodega of Santiago Ruiz, one of the most intriguing aspects of the wine is the bottle's label, which is a drawing of a route to a local wedding.

BODEGAS IN RIAS BAIXAS

Agnus Dei [E4]
Axis, Simes, Meaño
36968 Pontevedra
Tel: +351 223 746 660
sandramarques@calem.pt
This winery doesn't sell to the public.

As Laxas [B2]
A Laxas 16, 36430 Arbo
Tel: +34 986 665 444
Mobile (Simeón):
+34 618 788 165
export@bodegasaslaxas.com
www.bodegasaslaxas.com
The website has a map with directions to the bodega.

Castro Martin [E4]
Puxafeita 3
36636 Ribadumia
Tel: +34 986 710 202
info@bodegascastromartin.com
www.bodegascastromartin.com

Granja Fillaboa [B3]
Lugar de Fillaboa
36459 Salvaterra do Miño
Tel: +34 986 658 132
info@bodegasfillaboa.com
www.fillaboa.es

Lagar de Fornelos [A4]
B° de Cruces s/n
Fornelos
36778 O Rosal
Tel: +34 986 625 875
lagar@jet.es
www.riojalta.com

La Val [A4]
San Miguel de Tabagón 19
36760 O Rosal
Tel: +34 986 610 728
rebeca@terranostravinos.com

Martín Códax [E4]
Burgáns 91
Vilariño
36633 Cambados
Tel: +34 986 526 040
commercial@martincodax.com
www.martincodax.com

continued over the page

BODEGAS IN RIAS BAIXAS (CONTINUED)

Marqués de Vizhoja [B2]
Finca la Moreira
36430 Arbo, Pontevedra
Tel: +34 986 665 825
marquesdevizhoja@marquesd
evizhoja.com
www.marquesdevizhoja.com

Palacio de Fefiñanes [E4]
Pl Fefiñáns s/n
36630 Cambados
Tel: +34 986 542 204
fefinan@arrakis.es

Pazo de Señoráns [F4]
Vilanoviña
36616 Meis
Tel: +34 986 715 373
senorans@retemail.es

Pazo San Mauro [B3]
Porto s/n
36458 Salvaterra de Miño
Tel: +34 986 658 285

Santiago Ruiz [A4]
Rúa do Viticultor S. Ruiz
San Miguel de Tabagón
36760 O Rosal
Tel: +34 986 614 083
info@bodegasantiagoruiz.com
www.bodegasantiagoruiz.com

Terras Gauda [A4]
Ctra Tui – A Guarda (km 46)
36760 O Rosal
Tel: +34 986 621 001
terrasgauda@terrasgauda.com
www.terrasgauda.com

Valmiñor [A4]
A Portela s/n
San Juan de Tabagón
36760 O Rosal
Tel: +34 986 609 060
valminor@adegasvalminor.com
www.adegasvalminor.com

RIGHT *The parador in Monforte de Lemos is housed in a 17th-century Benedictine monastery.*

A modern approach

Having dropped down to A Guarda for lunch at one of the harbour-side eateries, make your way back up the PO553 to Fornelos and Lagar de Fornelos, which is just north of the town. This forward thinking bodega is the first in the region to bottle its wine under screwcap (for the UK market only), an obvious choice of closure for a fresh, fruity wine such as Albariño, yet one that most growers in this highly traditional region won't even consider. The wine, Lagar de Cervera, is 100% Albariño and packed with deliciously vibrant apricot and lemon fruit. You can visit between 9am and noon, Monday to Friday.

From here the route continues north to the little coastal town of Oia, where you can stop off to look at the monastery with its impressive baroque façade. The drive from here up to Baiona is lovely and for stunning ocean views you'll need to book yourself into the Parador de Baiona for the night.

Tui to Ribadavia

Route Three heads east into the Condado do Tea sub-zone, which follows the northern bank of the Río Miño almost as far as Ribadavia.

Beginning at La Val (the bodega is signposted off the road which runs from Salceda de Caselas to Salvaterra de Miño), your second stop is in nearby Porto, around 10km (6 miles) from Tui and just after Caldelas. Here you'll find the beautifully situated Pazo San Mauro, with stunning views across the river to Portugal and a chapel dating from 1592. A little further on is Granja Fillaboa at Arantel, and further still As Laxas at Arbo.

As I write, As Laxas is in the process of building a restaurant, so by the time you visit it'll be a good place to stop off for lunch and a glass or two of the spicy, tropical Bagoa do Mino.

Last stop

The last stop on this route is Marqués de Vizhoja, whose wine is officially Vino de la Tierra de Galicia rather than DO Rías Baixas, as it contains just 60% Albariño rather than the 70% stipulated by the DO. Continue up to Ribadavia for the night (*see p.51* for more about the town).

Fire water

Many of the bodegas also produce grape brandy or *eau de vie*, which is known as "orujo" in Galicia. Although it used to be pretty rough stuff, you can now find some very good examples which are often flavoured with herbs or coffee. The orujo is usually stylishly packaged and can therefore make rather nice presents.

Ribeiro and Ribeira Sacra

In venturing into Ribeiro and Ribeira Sacra you're entering Galicia's less visited interior, where river valleys replace coastal resorts, vineyards surround ancient architectural treasures, and the splendours of rural Spain are more immediate than ever. These are not, however, areas especially used to wine tourists, and if you don't speak the language, you may have to be flexible about what you manage to achieve. But for every small frustration I guarantee you'll make an exciting discovery.

Wine history

We're now in the province of Ourense and considering Ribeiro is one of the oldest DO regions in Spain, it seems amazing that we know so little about it. The fact is that until recently it was a victim of its own success. For many years it was an exporter of bulk wines, latterly made from the characterless Palomino variety, of which there are still sizeable plantations. When markets demanded more interesting white wines and competition from the New World became a reality, Ribeiro was unwilling, and in many ways unable, to respond.

All that is now finally changing. Palomino is not a recommended variety and experimentation with superior grape varieties such as Albariño, Treixadura, Torrontés, and Godello is widespread. There is a small amount of red wine produced here, but the majority is white wine, which may not quite match the quality of Rías Baixas, but it's certainly a good deal cheaper. Today the total vineyard area is approximately 3,000ha and there are around 35 bodegas making wine on a commercial scale.

Ribadavia

This charming town, which sits on a hillside surrounded by woods and vineyards, is the hub of the Ribeiro DO and was once home to one of the most prosperous Jewish communities in Spain. It's thanks to the thousands of Jews who lived and worked here, mostly involved in the wine business, that many improvements were made in vineyard techniques from the 11th to the 15th centuries. Today the Barrio Xudeo (Jewish Quarter) is just one

continued on p.55

of the many interesting stops you can make on a wander through the town's old stone streets.

Getting there
Again you're likely to have flown into Santiago de Compostela, and you can catch a train to Vigo from there if you'd prefer to keep driving to a minimum. However, although there are regional trains and buses which head east to Ribadavia, Ourense, and Monforte, you'll need a car to cover the suggested wine routes in Ribeiro and Ribeira Sacra. You can arrange to pick up a hire car in Vigo through www.carhireexpress.co.uk.

Travelling Around
Route One summary This route begins in Leiro and drops down to Ribadavia via Beade, before continuing east to Barbantes. The route is around 25km (15.5 miles).
Route Two summary This route begins in A Ponte (Arnoia) and heads up and east along the southern banks of the river to Puga. The route is 18km (11.2 miles).
Note: You could join the two routes together and make them into one long route by crossing over the river from Barbantes to Puga and following route two in reverse.

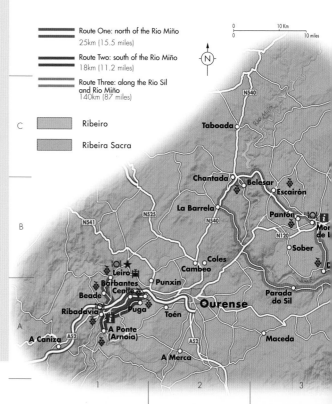

Route One: north of the Río Miño

Leiro sits surrounded by vineyards on the banks of the river Avia. One of the two most important bodegas in the region, Viña Meín, is here. This estate is owned by a lawyer, Javier Alén, who planted vines here in the late 1980s and who now also has a bodega and a lovely little rural hotel. Situated as Viña Meín is, just behind the Monasterio de San

ABOVE *Monforte's 16th-century bridge over the Río Cabe.*

Clodio (see the map on the website, www.vinamein.com) and close to the Oenological Station of Galicia, it's the perfect spot to base yourself whilst you explore the other local bodegas.

The estate makes a red wine from a blend which includes the virtually unknown Caiño Longo and Ferrón grape varieties, as well as two whites, one barrel fermented, and both from 80% Treixadura with Loureira, Godello, Torrontés, Albariño, and Lado.

From Leiro drop down towards Ribadavia via Beade, where A Portela produces *orujo* (grape brandy) in natural, herb, and coffee flavours, as well as a range of four wines.

Your next stop is the town of Ribadavia, where you'll find Vitivinícola de Ribeiro. This large cooperative winery was created in 1967 and has been responsible for leading the way in terms of technological advancements in the region. Today it produces around 40% of all Ribeiro wine and its white Viña Costeira, which doesn't look terribly promising from the label, is in fact a deliciously fruity blend of Torrontés, Treixadura, and Godello. Stock up while you can.

A little east of here, at Barbantes, is one of a string of 12 wineries throughout the whole of Spain that are owned by Bodegas y Bebidas. Built in an old picture house, Bodegas Alanís has been in existence since 1910 and although today it's owned by a large group, it still manages to have a small-scale and unglamorous feel to it.

BODEGAS IN RIBERIRO (CONTINUED)

Viña Meín [B1]
Lugar de Meín
32420 San Clodio, Leiro
Tel: +34 988 488 400
Mobile (Ricardo): +34 617
326 248 for visits.
vinamein@wol.es
www.vinamein.com
(See website for map)

Vitivinícola de Ribeiro [A1]
32415 Valdepereira
Ribadavia, Ourense
Tel: +34 988 477 210
pazo@pazoribeiro.com
www.vinoribeiro.com

WHERE TO STAY

For spa hotels in the
region of Ourense see
www.caldaria.es
Look out for the 4-star
Hotel Abadía de Arnoia, a
beautiful old converted priory.

Balneario de Arnoia [A1]
C/Vila Termal 1, Arnoia
32417 Ourense
Tel: +34 988 492 400
This 3-star hotel is close to
Ribadavia and has a good
restaurant. Plus for a price
they'll smear you in mud.

Monasterio de San Clodio
[B1] San Clodio
32427 Leiro
Tel: +34 988 485 601
www.turgalicia.com
www.ecoturismorural.com
See website for a map.
This has a good restaurant.

Viña Meín [B1]
See box above for details.
A rural hotel with 6 rooms
costing €60 per room per
night, including breakfast.

Route Two: south of the Río Miño

This route begins in very civilized fashion, with a spot of pampering. If you go onto the website (www.caldaria.es) you'll find a small chain of spa hotels, one of which is located in Arnoia, just south of Ribadavia. Here you can spend a couple of days cleansing body and soul before you get down to the serious work of sampling the local wines.

The route is a simple one which heads east following the south bank of the Río Miño as far as Puga. There are just a couple of suggested wineries and the first is the eponymously named Emilio Rojo. The winery was established in 1987 by an engineer turned winemaker determined to grow only local varieties on his 2ha estate. Sr Rojo concentrates all his efforts on just one top-quality white wine, Emilio Rojo, which is a blend of Treixadura, Loureiro, Torrontés, Albariño, and Lado.

From here take the OU402 across to Puga and Bodegas Campante. This larger estate, with its smart "white box" winery, was founded in the 1940s and produces both white and red wines from the local varieties already mentioned.

Ribeira Sacra

Having "seen the sea" in Rías Baixas and ambled around ancient ruins in Ribeiro, it's now time for some stunning scenery in Ribeira Sacra. The pretty old town of Monforte de Lemos is at the heart of this wine region and its imposing parador, a converted 17th-century Benedictine monastery, is the place to stay. If you've just about had your fill of crisp and refreshing Galician white wines, you'll be pleased to hear that vino tinto features prominently on the menu in Ribeira Sacra, usually made from the local Mencía grape, and with a welcome emphasis on quality rather than quantity.

Getting there

See p.52.

Travelling around

Route Three summary From Monforte de Lemos this route heads northwest towards Chantada via Pantón and Escairón. At Chantada the route drops down south on the N540 taking an almost immediate detour round by Belesar. At Barrela you take a left and drop down through the Gargantas del Sil until another left turning will bring you to Doade and from here you complete the circle by heading back up to Monforte. This route is 140km (87 miles), so you might like to spread the journey over two days.

Route Three: along the Río Sil and Río Miño

The Ribeira Sacra wine region has five sub-zones that cling to the banks of the rivers Sil and Miño. This may make for backbreaking work in the vineyards, but it also gives the vines good growing conditions, as they benefit from favourable exposure to the sun and protection from cold winds. In 2005 there were 99 registered *adegas* and 1,270ha under vine.

Beginning in Monforte de Lemos the route first heads east to Pantón and Adegas San José. Here both red and white wines are made from the favoured Mencía and Godello varieties. Godello is a grape that you rarely see outside of Galicia, yet it's recently started to yield some delicious wines, full of rich citric flavours and crisp, juicy acidity.

Continuing on up towards Chantada take a detour via Escairón and the village of A Cova, where you'll find Adegas Moure (this is difficult to find so ring ahead for directions). Although you may not be invited to take a dip in the pool, you will have the opportunity to buy some of the best wines in the region, again both red and white made from Mencía, Godello, and Albariño.

As you drop down from Chantada head towards Belesar and visit Adegas e Viñedos Vía Romana. Although some of the other wineries may not offer tourist visits, this *adega* certainly does. The winery was established in 1997 and makes only red wine from, you guessed it, Mencía.

The route now heads southeast to the confluence of the Río Sil and Río Miño. From here the drive along the Gargantas del Sil (Sil Gorges) doesn't have anything to do with wine, but it's absolutely breathtaking and not to be missed. Our final stop is just outside Doade as you complete the circular drive back up to Monforte de Lemos. Regina Viarum is another producer dedicated solely to Mencía and the grapes from its riverside vineyards are used to make two red wines, Viña Imperial and Regina Viarum.

BODEGAS IN RIBEIRA SACRA

Adegas Moure [B/C3]
Avda Buenos Aires12
Escairón – O Saviño
27540 Lugo
Tel: +34 982 452 031
abadiadacova@
adegasmoure.com
www.adegasmoure.com

Adegas San José [B3]
Santa Mariña de Eiré
Pantón
27439 Lugo
Tel: +34 982 456 545
abegas@infonegocio.com

**Adegas e Viñedos
Vía Romana [B/C2]**
A Ermida
Belesar, Chantada
27514 Lugo
Tel: +34 982 462 069
viaromana@viaromana.es

Rectoral de Amandi [B3]
Amandi – Sober
vinos@bodegasgallegas.com
www.bodegasgallegas.com

Regina Viarum [B3]
Doade, Sober
27427 Lugo
Tel: +34 619 009 777
clients@reginaviarum.es
www.reginaviarum.es

USEFUL INFORMATION

**Oficina de Turismo
Monforte de Lemos**
La Casitas de la
Compañia s/n
27400 Monforte de Lemos
Tel: +34 982 404 715

www.ribeirasacra.org
For information on the DO.

LEFT *Ribeira's Viña Meín is one of the few wineries which also has a small rural hotel.*

The three Chacolís

I'm sure you've heard of Bilbao. It's likely that the city's Guggenheim Museum is also familiar, whether you've stepped inside its gleaming metallic exterior or not. How about the Chacolís? No? Given that this delightful little wine region surrounds and spills out from one of Spain's most exciting cities, why on earth don't more people know about it?

Route One: Chacolí de Guetaria
108km (67 miles)

Route Two: Chacolí de Vizcaya and Alava
70km (44 miles)

0   5   10 Km
0   5   10 miles

Venture into the rural north

Admittedly, visiting the Chacolís as a wine tourist demands a spirit of adventure and a highly developed sense of curiosity. But more than either of these, a love of lip-smackingly fresh white wine is what's really required. A smattering of Spanish will come in useful too, as this is rural winemaking country where wines are made from grapes most of us have never even heard of, by small, family-run wineries dotted throughout the rolling hills that cling to the cool Atlantic coastline. The countryside is lush and green, the pace of

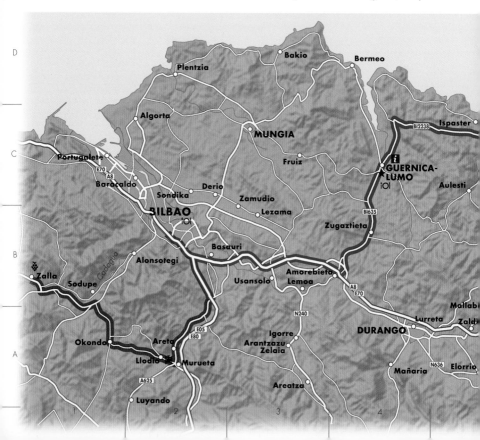

life reassuringly slow. And, quite honestly, I can't imagine anything more perfect than sitting in the balmy evening air of Guetaria with the sound of the sea lapping beneath you as you tuck into a plate of freshly barbecued fish and a glass of chilled Chacolí wine.

Proud to be Basque
This is Basque Country, "*País Vasco*", and the Basques are a resolutely individual people. Nowhere is this more apparent than in their language, "*Euskara*", which, in spite of hefty opposition, they've managed to preserve for thousands of years. It's a language like no other and when you see it for the first time it can seem daunting. However, if you simply remember that "tx" is pronounced "ch" you'll be amazed how far it will get you.

What is Basque Country?
The Basques are an ancient nation whose country is defined by culture rather than modern national boundaries. Thus, part of the Basque Country is in France and part in Spain, as with Catalonia.

This is a unique and disparate wine area, known as "the Chacolís" because there are three separate Chacolí regions which fall into three Basque provinces, Guipúzcoa, Vizcaya, and Alava. Each has its own DO, with Alava being a recent 2003 addition.

ABOVE *The grand house at Virgen de Lorea in Zalla.*

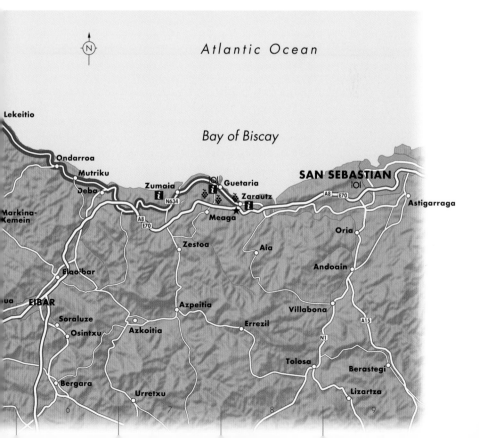

ABOVE *In the coastal areas of Galicia and the Chacolís, most vines are trained on pergolas.*

WHERE TO EAT

Berton [B2]
Jardines 11
48009 Bilbao
Tel: +34 944 167 035

Café Iruña [B2]
Jardines de Albia
48009 Bilbao
Tel: +34 944 237 021

Elkano [C7/8]
C/Herrerieta 2
20808 Guetaria
Tel: +34 943 140 614

Legoie (*pincho* bar) [C4]
Barrenkalea
48300 Guernica

Mayflower Restaurant [C7/8] Katrapona, 4
20808 Guetaria
Tel: +34 943 140 658

Victor Montes [B2]
Plaza Nueva 8
48005 Bilbao
Tel: +34 944 155 603
www.bilbaoweb.com/victormontes

Guipúzcoa, which occupies the eastern corner and coastline of the area, has 177ha under vine and its wines are known as "Chacolí de Guetaria" ("Getariako Txakolina"). Those from Vizcaya (140ha under vine) are known as "Chacolí de Vizcaya" ("Bizkaiko Txakolina") and come from six zones to the west, spread out around the city of Bilbao. And finally there's Alava (60ha under vine), which covers a small area south of Bilbao, whose wines are known as "Chacolí de Alava" ("Arabako Txakolina") – this province also encompasses part of Rioja DOCa.

Unique drinking

If the language and country are unique then exactly the same can be said of the wines. To begin with the two main grape varieties, Hondarrabi Zuri (white) and Hondarrabi Beltza (red), are grown only in the Basque Country. Around 85% of the vineyard area is planted to Hondarrabi Zuri and although a small amount of rosé and red wine is produced, the large majority is white wine, made from a blend of the two varieties (the juice of both white and red grapes is always white, it's only when you leave it in contact with the red grape skins that it takes on any colour).

The Chacolís receive plenty of rainfall so, to avoid vines getting soggy feet, many of the coastal vineyards are planted on slopes. That way excess rainwater drains away whilst the vines have maximum exposure to the sun. Training is usually on pergolas which allow the drying wind to pass through more easily – an important consideration in a humid climate, where fungal disease is always a potential hazard. Pergola training systems also protect the grapes from getting sunburnt in the height of a hot summer.

The key to making good Chacolí wine is to retain as much fruit and freshness as possible. This is done through swift and minimal handling of the grapes and temperature-controlled fermentation in stainless-steel tanks. The creamy flavour of the lees (dead yeast cells) is also important for the finished wine, so the fermented juice can remain with these from February until bottling in September.

The final style is very distinctive: crisp and lemony with a hint of cream, a slightly salty tang, and a lingering flavour of dried wild herbs. It's similar to good Muscadet with an added touch of spritz. It's also a wine made to be drunk from the moment it's bottled, so don't plan on carting it home to collect dust in the under-stairs cupboard for the next 10 years, either drink it there and then or enjoy it on a regular basis for up to six months after you return.

As you move further south into the inland areas of Vizcaya and Alava the climate is a little hotter and you'll notice the wines tend to be fuller, peachier, spicier even, and slightly more alcoholic.

Arranging a visit

Few wineries here are big on exporting (exceptions include Txomin Etxaniz and Ametzoi), so virtually any wine you try is going to be a brand new taste experience. Even in the unlikely event of you having tried some Chacolí wine at home, it will taste better in Spain as it won't have undergone the heavy filtering necessary to keep it stable during its journey overseas.

The suggested routes mapped out below include visits to just a couple of the largest bodegas with the most impressive wines, but even these may prove difficult to arrange if you don't speak Spanish. Whatever you do, don't despair! If all else fails just pick up a map of the local bodegas from the tourist office in Guetaria or Zarautz and drive around taking a look at them – you never know, you may bump into a friendly winemaker keen for your business and not too worried whether he understands you or not. If cycling along the picturesque coastal road appeals, then you can hire bicycles in Zumaia for 3 euros a day.

Getting there

Both routes begin in Bilbao, with one heading out east along the coast and the other following a much shorter route south-west of the city. Because of the nature of the tiny places you'll be visiting, taking trains will be problematic and I'd suggest that hiring a car in Bilbao is really the only way to cover this area.

Travelling around

Route One summary Throughout this route your base will be the tiny fishing village of Guetaria, and the emphasis is on a relaxing seaside type of stay. The route heads out of Bilbao towards the coast via Guernica and then continues east to Guetaria and finally to Zarautz. It's around an hour and a half's drive (not allowing for stops) from Bilbao to Zarautz. The total journey is 108km (67 miles).

Route Two summary This heads south out of Bilbao to Llodio then across to Zalla via Okondo. It's a shorter route and at a gentle pace it should take you under an hour. The round trip back to Bilbao is around 70km (44 miles).

Route One: Chacolí de Guetaria

From Bilbao take the main A8/E70 motorway until you reach the junction with the B1635 which runs up towards the coast. Take this road until your first stop off in Guernica. Although there's nothing particularly wine related to be found here, it's the perfect place to brush up on Basque political history. It was here that the Basque independent parliament sat (underneath the famous ancient oak, whose trunk still stands in

BODEGAS IN THE CHACOLIS

Ametzoi [C7/8]
B° Eitzaga 10
20808 Guetaria
Tel: +34 943 140 918

Talai-Berri Txakolina [C8]
Talaimendi Auzoa 728
(Kanpinaren Indoan)
Apdo 184,
20800 Zarautz
Tel: +34 943 132 750
talaiberri@euskalnet.net

Txomin Etxaniz [C7/8]
20808 Guetaria
Tel: +34 943 140 702/
+34 629 015 865
www.txominetxaniz.com
txakoli@txominetxaniz.com

Virgen de Lorea [B1]
Juan de Ajuriaguerra 9–6
48009 Bilbao
Tel: +34 944 234 035
spankor@cnb.informail.es

BELOW *A ceramic tile replica of Picasso's* Guernica *on Calle Allende Salazar, Guernica – the original hangs in Madrid's Centro de Arte Reina Sofía.*

WHERE TO STAY

Gran Hotel Domine Bilbao [B2]
Alameda Mazarredo 61
48009 Bilbao
Tel: +34 944 253 300
www.granhotel
dominebilbao.com
From €175

Hostal Itxas-Gain [C7/8]
C/San Roque 1
20808 Guetaria
Tel: +34 943 141 033/5
€46

Landarte [C7/8]
Carretera Artadi 1
20750 Zumaia
Tel: +34 943 865 358
www.landarte.net
€65–75 including breakfast

Miró Hotel [B2]
Alameda Mazarredo 77
48009 Bilbao
Tel: +34 946 611 880
www.mirohotelbilbao.com
From €170

Pensión Guetariano [C7/8]
Herrerieta Kalea 3
20808 Guetaria
Tel: +34 943 140 567
€50

RIGHT *Sign at Virgen de Lorea.*

BELOW *The port at Guetaria.*

the gardens of the Casa de Juntas) until 1876. The town was also the scene of one of the most horrific bombing campaigns of the Spanish Civil War when in April 1937 General Francisco Franco (with help from Hitler's Condor Legion) virtually razed it as part of his unsuccessful attempt to eradicate the Basques. You'll find a copy of Picasso's Guernica, the artist's own interpretation of events, in the form of a large ceramic tile picture on Calle Allende Salazar.

Guernica's well-equipped tourist office (www.gernika-lumo.net) will be able to point you in the right direction for the various museums and places of historical interest within this now flourishing and rather lovely town.

If you find yourself in need of refreshment then just around the corner from the tourist office you'll find Lejoie, whose breaded bulls' testicles won it "best *pincho* bar in Bizkaia 2002", an award it took again in 2004 for a rather more conservative dish involving mushrooms. "*Pintxo*" (*pincho*) is the Basque word for a *tapa* and two or three of these washed down with an ice-cold beer are the perfect antidote to the blistering summer heat of Guernica's dusty streets.

Sleepy seafood

From Guernica head up to Lekeitio on the B12238 and from here follow the coastal road to Guetaria, stopping off at one or two of the little seaside towns along the way. Guetaria is a tiny medieval fishing village and accommodation comes in the form of a couple of modest *pensiones*, both perfectly comfortable and situated opposite each other in the centre of the village. If you're struggling to decide which to choose, perhaps the chance to breakfast on freshly squeezed orange juice and warm crusty baguette on a cliff-top overlooking the Atlantic may just tip the balance towards Hostal Itxas-Gain. There's no car park and the front door is at the bottom of a narrow side street so I'd suggest parking in any of the surrounding streets.

Guetaria boasts 10 of Chacolí de Guetaria's 17 bodegas and one of the best to visit is Txomin Etxaniz. Its owner, Ernesto Chueca, used to make his wine in a 14th-century building next to the church in Guetaria itself, but moved to new facilities just out of town when the business expanded. From the main square take the road towards Meaga which runs up the left side of restaurant Elkano. After a couple of kilometres (about a mile) you'll come to a crossroads where you turn left, towards Santa Barbara. The winery is the third turning on the left (just after the lookout point).

Fifth-generation Ernesto is a true local and doesn't speak any English. He makes 250,000 bottles a year, of which 50% is sold to restaurants in Spain. Some vines are over 100 years old, all are trained on pergolas, and hand harvesting takes place from the end of September. The views are stunning and the new "tourist area" should be finished by the time you read this. Txomin Etxaniz makes just one wine, a white, arguably the best from the region, and the perfect foil to a plate of salted anchovies or *bonito* (tuna).

The best way to try the local wines is to head for Guetaria's port (you may even catch the locals playing an early evening game of *pelota* on the way) and one of its cosy little seafood eateries. You'll find most of the local producers on the wine list and you shouldn't expect to pay more than 10 euros per bottle.

Bathing, bronzing, and boozing

As you drive the 5km (3 miles) from Guetaria to Zarautz you'll be surrounded by vineyards all the way. In Zarautz you'll find the longest beach on the Guipúzcoa coast being enjoyed by tourists and locals alike. Although today this is a cosmopolitan tourist town with ice-cream parlours, surfers, and smart hotels, its history dates back to the 13th century and the Art and History Museum (tel: +34 943 835 281) is the place to find out all about it. But we're here for the wine and if you take either a drive, cycle ride (*see* Zumaia tourist office for cycle hire), or walk towards the main campsite ("Gran Camping"), you'll come across Talai-Berri who offers tours from 9am-1pm daily (9 euros and you must book in advance). One of the better bodegas of the area, it also makes fiery *aguardiente* to help digest all that delicious fish.

Route Two: Chacolí de Vizcaya and Alava

Bilbao is perhaps best known for its stunning Guggenheim Museum and a trip to the city really wouldn't be complete without a visit to American architect Frank Gehry's masterpiece. But on a recent trip I also found that the old town, "*casco viejo*", was wonderful, with lots of tiny streets peppered with crusty old bars serving authentic *tapas* to locals and tourists alike. For accommodation I've suggested a couple of ultra-trendy new hotels just across from the Guggenheim which I feel offer far better value than the faded grandeur of the formerly glamorous Carlton, or, at the other extreme, the shabbily decorated, lino-floored grimness of most budget options.

Driving out of Bilbao can, as with most large cities, prove challenging, but aim to head south on the main E05/A68 motorway as far as junction one, where you need to pick up the B1625 down to Llodio. Here you're in the province of Alava and there's a fascinating museum of gastronomy to visit (*see* the box over the page for details).

USEFUL INFORMATION

Turismo Guetaria
Aldamar Parkea 2
20808 Guetaria
Tel: +34 943 140 957
getaria@nauta.es

Turismo Guernica
Artekalea 8
48300 Guernica-Lumo
Tel: +34 946 255 892
turismo@gernika-lumo.net
www.gernika-lumo.net

Turismo Zarautz
Avda Navarra
20800 Zarautz
Tel: +34 943 830 990
turismoa@zarautz.org
www.turismozarautz.com

Turismo Zumaia
1 Zuloaga Enparantza
20750 Zumaia
Tel: +34 943 143 396
turismoa@zumaia.net
www.zumaia.net
A very helpful tourist office with a good website – click **turismoa** at the top for the English version. It offers everything from bicycle hire to organized walking tours and tailor-made excursions for visitors.

EXTRA INFORMATION
. . . .
Getariako Txakolina DO
Parque Aldamar 4 Bajo
20808 Getaria
Tel: +34 943 140 383
rmozo@getariakotxakolina.com
www.getariakotxakolina.com

Museum of Gastronomy
[A2] Zubiko Etxea Maestro
Elorza 11
01400 Llodio
Alava
Tel: +34 946 724 330
Entrance: free.
5.30–8.30pm Fri, Sat;
11am–2pm Sun and
holidays; visit by prior
arrangement 10am–2pm
Thu and Fri.

www.alavaincoming.com
for organized gastronomic
tours of the region.

**www.basquecountry-
tourism.**com includes
information on **custom or
ready-made tours,** such as
a hike along Guipúzcoa's
coast followed by a
refreshing glass of Txacolí,
or a three-hour *pincho*
tour of San Sebastián.

www.gipuzkoaturismo.net
is a useful website for
finding out about
Guipúzcoan food and
accommodation.

www.nekatur.net
is a good for finding rural
guesthouses and farmhouse
accommodation throughout
the Basque Country.

Follow the road west out of Llodio to Okondo, then continue on up and along the banks of the river Cadagua to Zalla. In Zalla take the right-hand fork towards "Otxaran/Muebles el Paraiso" and when you spy a whole host of vines you'll soon also see Virgen de Lorea to your right.

The house in front of the winery, with its deep terracotta walls, sweeping front stairways, and galleried second-floor balcony, looks like a palace from a Disney film and is quite something to behold. It's the home of owner and furniture magnate Cosme Vivanco Arístarán, who makes two wines, both white, neither of which are exported – so make the most of your visit and try them while you can. The more expensive Señorio de Otxaran (around 6 euros) is the better wine and reminiscent of a powerful, spritzy Pinot Grigio. This is Chacolí de Vizcaya of course and the slightly warmer microclimate results in wines which are waxier and more mouth-filling than the coastal wines of Chacolí de Guetaria. Hopefully when you visit, the brand new winery will be finished.

Reaching for the stars
Although the wines and the countryside are wonderful, it's impossible to leave the Basque Country without mentioning its food. Guipúzcoa alone boasts 15 Michelin stars and a strong gastronomic tradition imbues every aspect of Basque life. In San Sebastián, east of Zarautz, you'll find some of the best *pincho* bars in Spain, along with Juan Mari Arzak's eponymous Michelin-starred restaurant (tel: +34 943 278 465/+34 943 285 593; email: restaurante@arzak.es; www.arzak.es). But wherever you go, from the tiniest little seafront eatery where the fish is tossed onto an open-air griddle and charred to perfection in front of your eyes, to some of the smartest restaurants in Northern Spain, the food will always be good.

Ploughman's lunch
The area's best-known cheese is *idiazabal*, made in a town of the same name southwest of San Sebastián. It has a firm, creamy texture, and is made from the milk of the Latxa sheep. You can buy it young, aged, or smoked, and the one with the black label is the best.

Cider was made here long before wine and in January there's great excitement as the cider houses throw open their doors and the first tastings of the season begin. Cider is the most popular drink in Guipúzcoa and in many a local bar you can watch as the fresh brew is theatrically poured from a great height. This apparently releases all of the heady, appley aromas and flavours as the liquid splashes against the side of the glass. The town of Astigarraga just southeast of San Sebastián is the most famous for its cider production.

Rioja

Rioja is without question one of the most beautiful wine regions in the world. Majestic grey mountain-tops, rugged sandy slopes, fields of golden sunflowers, and oceans of squat green vines seem to follow you wherever you go. Rioja is also, of course, the name of one of the most famous wines in the world, and to try to tell you everything there is to know about it would take up this whole book and more. As there are several excellent volumes already published on the subject I'm going to leave that research up to you. What I will tell you is that Rioja is one of Spain's most advanced regions when it comes to wine tourism, and although I've included a lot of visitor-friendly bodegas on the routes below, there are many more for you to discover.

The basics
• In 1925 Rioja became the first officially demarcated wine region in Spain.
• In 1991 Rioja was the first area to be awarded the superior DOCa. In 2003 it was joined by Priorat and to this day they remain the only two regions with this classification.
• Red wines are made from Tempranillo (61% of the total DOCa Rioja vineyard area), Garnacha, Mazuelo, and Graciano, with Cabernet Sauvignon still classed as an "experimental" variety.
• White wines are mostly made from Viura, with Malvasía Riojana and Garnacha Blanca occasionally playing a part in the blend.
• The terms *jóvenes*, *crianza*, *reserva*, and *gran reserva* are not an indication of quality, only a guarantee of the minimum time a given wine has spent in oak and bottle.
• The region is split into three winemaking sub-zones:
Rioja Alta – to the west and below the Río Ebro;
Rioja Alavesa – west and above the Río Ebro;
Rioja Baja – east, up to the border with Navarra.

Four top years
Since the official recognition of the denomination of Rioja in 1925 only 10 harvests have been rated as "excellent" – 1994, 1995, 2001, and the recent 2004 vintages are all in the top 10.

Rioja has over 2,500 bodegas with a total of 58,117ha of vines in production. Of the 356 million

BELOW *It is hard to imagine the hot Spanish sun above when you are down in a cool cellar.*

RIGHT *Logroño's central market is the ideal place to buy cured meats and cheeses, as well as to wonder at the array of fresh fish and local vegetables.*

Rioja Alta

Rioja Baja

Navarra

Rioja Alavesa

Route One: Rioja Alavesa
94km (58 miles)

Route Two: Rioja Alta
15km (9 miles)

Route Three: Rioja Alta
27km (17 miles)

Route Four: Rioja Baja
75km (46.5 miles) d

bottles of DOCa Rioja produced annually, just over 90% are red, almost 6% are white, and 4% rosé.

High tradition versus high expression

In the traditional winemaking of Rioja, a selection of grapes from the three sub-zones are blended together to produce a balanced wine representative of Rioja, rather than being the expression of a particular vineyard plot, microclimate, and/or variety.

Today these wines still account for the majority of the region's production, but they've been joined by a new wave of elite wines that have come to be known as *alta expresión*. Often produced from single-vineyard plots with old, low-yielding vines, these wines are made with all the loving care and expensive attention to detail that it's possible for a winemaker to lavish. Some people argue they are not "true Rioja" and have no sense of place. Others, myself included, relish the diversity they offer to a region that is currently producing better wines than ever before, at all levels, and in a fascinating array of styles.

As you travel around you'll encounter many great wines which fall somewhere between tradition and *alta expresión*, but to highlight the difference between these two particular extremes, I've chosen one of the very best traditional wines for you to pit against three of the most exciting new-wave examples.

Both here and within the routes mapped out below, I make no apology for suggesting expensive wines for you to buy. The fact is that in most local bars when you ask for a glass of wine you'll be given basic red *crianza* – the perfect accompaniment to a plate of *jamón* or *manchego*. On winery tours there'll be a

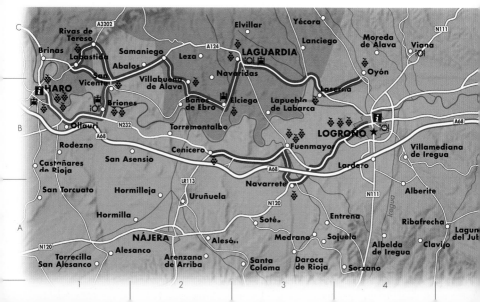

highly drinkable glass of *reserva* included in the price. Both *crianza* and *reserva* wines can be great value for money, so when you find one you like, see if it's for sale. Here, however, are some of the top of the crop.

Traditional
Castillo Ygay Gran Reserva Especial Tinto
This wine is the crowning glory of Marqués de Murrieta's original range. It's a classic blend of Tempranillo with Garnacha, Mazuelo, and Graciano, and spends no less than four years ageing in American oak – the result is a traditionalist's dream.

Alta expresión
Bodegas Lan (limited edition)
Although the blend of grapes in Lan is very similar to that of Ygay, the wines couldn't be more different. I'm going to stick my

USEFUL INFORMATION

Consejo Regulador (Rioja) [B4] Estambrera 52
26006 Logroño
Tel: +34 941 500 400
www.riojawine.com

La Enoteca (wine shop) [B1]
C/Arrabal 3, 26200 Haro
Tel: +34 941 313 086
Almost 200 Riojas in stock.

Museo de La Rioja [B4]
Plaza de San Agustín
26001 Logroño
Tel: +34 941 291 259
10am–2pm, 4–9pm
Tue–Sat; 11.30am–2pm
Sun; closed Mon.

Tourist Offices:
Alfaro
Argelillo 7, 26540 Alfaro
Tel: +34 941 180 032
Calahorra
Angel Olivan 8
26500 Calahorra
Tel: +34 941 146 398
Haro
Plaza Monseñor Florentino
Rodríguez, 26200 Haro
Tel: +34 941 303 366
Logroño
Paseo del Espolón 1
26071 Logroño
Tel: +34 941 291 260
www.larioja.org (has visiting details for many bodegas.)

Parking in Logroño
There's a convenient but expensive underground car park in El Espalón. Tip: you can park on the street for free after 8.30pm.

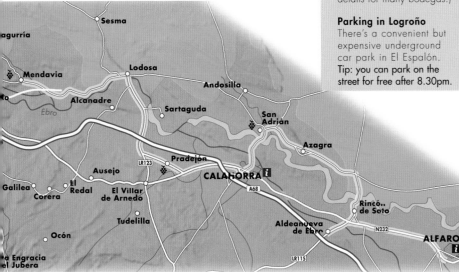

WHERE TO STAY
. . . .

Castillo El Collado [C3]
Paseo El Collado 1
01300 Laguardia
Tel: +34 945 621 200
hcastillocollado@euskalnet.net
www.euskalnet.net/hotelcollado
€110 for a double.
There's a very good
restaurant here too.

**Hotel Marqués de Vallejo
[B4]** Marqués de Vallejo 8
26001 Logroño
Tel: +34 941 248 333
info@hotelmarquesdevallejo.com
www.hotelmarquesdevallejo.com
From €90 for a double.

RIGHT *Wire-trained vines.*

BELOW *After phylloxera hit
France, many Riojan wineries
built railway stations to meet
increased distribution needs.*

neck on the line and, having evaluated this wine blind on at least three occasions, I'm going to declare it the best *alta expresión* wine to date.

Finca Allende Aurus
All the wines in this line-up contain between 80% and 100% Tempranillo, and Aurus is no exception. In Aurus it's an 85:15 split with Graciano and the wine spends two years in French oak before being bottled unfiltered. Like Lan, it's rich, dark, and utterly delicious.

Roda 1
Roda I is aromatic, silky, and seductive. If you can't afford it then Roda II is a good second best – and if you can afford it why not go the extra mile and buy a bottle of the flagship Cirsión?

Getting there
Easyjet (www.easyjet.com) flies from London Stansted to Bilbao and BA/Iberia (www.ba.com) co-chair flights there from London Heathrow. From Bilbao it's a straightforward 150km (93-mile) run on the A68/E05 motorway to Logroño. An alternative, to avoid the last stretch of the motorway, is to pick up the national N124 just north of Miranda de Ebro. A limited train service runs from Bilbao to Logroño (3–4 hours) and the regional R28 line links Haro, Briones, Cenicero, Logroño, and Alfaro (www.renfe.es).

Travelling around

Route One summary The route begins in Oyón and heads west towards Laguardia. It then drops down to Elciego and up, via Villabuena de Alava, to San Vicente de la Sonsierra. From here it loops around by Labastida and Rivas de Tereso before returning east to Laguardia. Approximately 94km (58 miles).

Route Two summary The first route in Rioja Alta begins in San Vicente de la Sonsierra and drops down immediately to Briones. It then heads west and finishes in Haro. Approximately 15km (9 miles).

Route Three summary The second route in Rioja Alta covers an area closer to Logroño and begins in Cenicero. From here it heads east to Fuenmayor, south to Navarrete and finally east to Logroño. Approximately 27km (17 miles).

Route Four summary Beginning in Mendavia, route four travels a twisting course east towards Navarra, via Lodosa, Pradejón, San Adrián, Aldeanueva de Ebro, and Alfaro. Approximately 75km (46.5 miles).

Route One: Rioja Alavesa

This is a long and beautiful drive through Rioja Alavesa, and I'd suggest that you break the journey into a two day trip. Beginning in Oyón, Bodegas Valdemar is part of Martínez Bujanda, a family-run group of four wineries that was founded in Oyón in 1889. The original bodega is now a museum full of old winemaking tools that today seem highly primitive in comparison with Rioja's ultra-modern installations. There are three ranges of wines, with Inspiración Valdemar being the newest and most exclusive. The two initial Inspiración wines are shortly to be joined by a third, made from a rare Riojan variety called Maturana, which for curiosity's sake alone must be tried.

Just along the road (A3226) the route takes a little detour via Laserno where you'll find a bodega belonging to the CVNE group. Contino is the company's prized 62ha single vineyard estate with cellars dating from the 15th century. If you're after good, classic Rioja, made from a blend of traditional grapes, then Contino's *crianza*, *reserva* and *gran reserva* wines certainly fit the bill. If, however, you want to try something more unusual, the Contino Graciano, with its deep purple hue and ripe, spicy aromas, is perhaps a more interesting wine.

Rioja revolution

Old meets avant-garde at Marqués de Riscal, the route's next bodega – take the A124 up to Laguardia and pick up the A3210 down to Elciego. You might even want to spend a night in the new luxury hotel here (*see* the box on p.70). The story of Don Camilo Hurtado de Amezaga, the Marqués de Riscal, is one of the most crucial chapters in Rioja's history, as it was he

(*see* the box on p.70)

WHERE TO EAT

Angel Bar [B4]
Calle del Laurel,
26001 Logroño
This bar serves only good, hot, garlicky mushrooms.

Bar San Juan [B4]
Calle San Juan
26001 Logroño
For sophisticated *tapas*.

La Chatilla de San Agustín [B4] San Agustín 6
26001 Logroño
Tel: +34 941 204 545
Try the carpaccio of *cigala*.

Leito's [B4]
Portales 30
26001 Logroño
Tel: +34 941 212 078
Set menu with wine, water, and bread, €22.

Mayor de Migueloa [C3]
Calle Mayor de Migueloa
01300 Laguardia
Tel: +34 945 621 175
Good *tapas* bar terrace.

Restaurant Borgia [C4]
C/Serapio Urra
31230 Viana
Tel: +34 948 645 781

ABOVE *Ysios (Route One) is the vision of architect Santiago Calatrava. It epitomizes Spain's new wave of design-led wineries.*

who brought Bordeaux casks, grapes, and know-how to the region in the mid-19th century, in a move that revolutionized Rioja's winemaking.

Visits here last around an hour and a half, cost 6 euros, and include a glass of *reserva* wine. The winery has a "library" of bottles dating back to its first vintage of 1862, and although that particular year isn't for sale, the *reserva* included in the tour – one of the bodega's best wines – certainly is.

As you drive up towards San Vicente de la Sonsierra you'll pass Villabuena de Alava, a sleepy little village with steep narrow streets, sandcoloured houses, and just 300 inhabitants. State-of-the-art Viña Izadi was established in 1987 and it's well worth a visit. Try Viña Izadi Expresión, a wine made from 70-year-old Tempranillo vines, that has won plaudits galore of late.

Just above Labastida on the road to Ribas de Tereso is Remelluri, an ancient property which once belonged to the monastery of Toloño. This attractive bodega with its own museum produces a small and consistently impressive range of wines. The blanco displays rich, ripe fruit that's in perfect balance with the toasted almond flavours of the oak. Of the four reds, the top-of-the-range Colección Jaime Rodriguez is a stunning, though expensive, wine.

From here it's time to make your way back to Laguardia for a couple more visits and a night in a mini-castle. Ysios, for its

architecture alone, is currently one of the most famous (and most photographed) bodegas in Rioja. Even if you choose not to visit, make sure you at least take a look at its exterior – there's a perfect view from the end of the walkway behind Castillo El Collado (*see* below). Bodegas Campillo is another winery owned by a group, this time the largest vineyard owner in Rioja, Grupo Faustino. A sweep of imposing black slate stairs leads dramatically up to this large and uniquely shaped white bodega – the jewel in the Faustino crown.

The place to stay in Laguardia is Castillo El Collado, with individually designed rooms, open stone walls, and its very own tower from which to survey this stunning region. Dining here you'll probably find that the man who has greeted you, shown you to your room, served you a drink, and seated you, is also your chef for the evening – I've never seen anyone work harder and his lamb cutlets are some of the best in Rioja.

Route Two: Rioja Alta via Haro

This is a much shorter route and focuses mainly on the town of Haro where several bodegas are located. The route begins directly east of the town in San Vicente de la Sonsierra, a village best remembered for its impressive medieval bridge. Here you'll find a clutch of wineries that includes Bodegas Sonsierra, a cooperative producing particularly good value for money *jóvenes* (young) wines.

Drop down from here to Briones on the LR210 (*see* Dinastía Vivanco, p.73). As well as boasting one of the finest wine museums in the world, Briones is also home to one of the newest and most forward-thinking wineries in Rioja, Finca Allende. This small family company was established in 1986 by winemaker Miguel Angel de Gregorio and his sister, Mercedes. In Gregorio's words, they wanted "to make wine for the heart, not only for the mouth", and, having carefully studied the terroir of the area, they gradually bought up small plots of suitable vineyard land. The first vintage for Allende was 1995, and to this day they make some

BODEGAS IN RIOJA

Route One
Bodegas Valdemar [B/C4]
Camino Viejo Logroño
01320 Oyón
Tel: +34 945 622 188
www.martinezbujanda.com

Campillo [C3]
C/de Logroño
01300 Laguardia
Tel: +34 945 600 826
www.bodegascampillo.es

Contino [C3]
Finca San Rafael, Laserna
01321 Laguardia
Tel: +34 945 600 201
www.cvne.com

Izadi [B2]
Viña Villabuena
Herreria Travesia 2 No 5
01307 Villabuena de Alava
Tel: +34 945 609 086
www.izadi.com

Marqués de Riscal [B2/3]
C/Torrea 1, 01340 Elciego
Tel: +34 945 606 000
www.marquesderiscal.com

Remelluri [C1]
01330 Labastida
Tel: +34 945 331 801
www.remelluri.com

Ysios [C3]
Camino de la Hoya
01300 Laguardia
Tel: +34 945 600 640
www.bodegasysios.com

Route Two
Bodegas Bilbaínas [B1]
Estación 3, 26200 Haro
Tel: +34 941 310 147
www.bodegasbilbainas.com

Bodegas Sonsierra [B1]
El Remedio
26338 San Vicente de
la Sonsierra
Tel: +34 941 334 031

continued on p.71

ARCHITECTURAL HIGHLIGHTS
· ·

Ysios – Architect **Santiago Calatrava's** only winery to date is extraordinary (*see* p.68). A shallow base of cedar wood topped with waves of shimmering roof. He also designed the magnificent bird-like airport at Bilbao.

Marqués de Riscal – **Frank Gehry's** "city of wine" includes a hotel, restaurant, and wine therapy spa. It is breathtaking and I imagine the residents of the sleepy little village of Elciego are wondering what's hit them.

López de Heredia – A wine shop rather than a winery, by **Zaha Hadid**, stands in stark contrast to the ultra-traditional winery.

BELOW *The beautiful sight of Rioja's sweeping sand-coloured vineyards bathed in sunshine.*

of the most modern, yet stylish wines in Rioja. The basic red *crianza* is superb, although the fruit from the estate's oldest vines is kept exclusively for Aurus and the new top *cuvée*, Calvario.

As you head into Haro follow the signs to the north of the town and you'll come across four major wineries; La Rioja Alta, Muga, Roda, and López de Heredia. All produce excellent wines, with Heredia's being the most traditional of the four. La Rioja Alta has managed to strike the difficult balance between continuing to produce old-style Rioja, whilst also freshening up its act to appeal to a broader audience. The family company of Muga has a history of winemaking which is firmly rooted in a love of wood. It makes all its own barrels and uses oak throughout the entire winemaking process. The wines are accordingly powerful and creamy. Roda is one of the most talked-about wineries of the moment and whether you choose to try Roda I, its lesser sibling Roda II, or the flagship Cirsión (over 100 euros a bottle), you'll be tasting some of Rioja's finest wine.

Bodegas Bilbaínas (*see* the map on its website, p.69) is just a short drive away and became part of the Codorníu group in 1997. A huge regeneration project is under way and it's well worth a visit to see what can be achieved when a run-down old bodega receives a large and thoughtfully utilized injection of cash. Visits here, which last an hour and a half and include a tasting of Viña Pomal Reserva, are free of charge and can be arranged for Sundays and public holidays. La Vicuana is one

of the best wines and is sold "*en rama*" or raw, which means the winemaker, José Hidalgo, has left it unfiltered with a view to achieving greater complexity.

Route Three: Rioja Alta via Logroño
The second Rioja Alta route begins in the town of Cenicero with a visit to another of Rioja's most famous bodegas, Marqués de Cáceres. It was Enrique Forner, son of a successful Bordeaux wine family, who created this estate under the guidance of Professor Emile Peynaud in the late 1960s. Together they introduced stainless-steel technology and the concept of shorter barrel-ageing to the region, in an attempt to produce wines that were fresher, cleaner, and more vibrant than had been known before. They succeeded and today the Cáceres wines are as popular as ever.

Heading east along the N232 you'll come to Fuenmayor, a town with three excellent bodegas that between them demonstrate perfectly the diversity of styles within Rioja today. Montecillo belongs firmly to the old school and produces wonderfully traditional wines that have an ability to age for decades. Finca Valpiedra is another of the Martínez Bujanda wineries and, interestingly enough, it was sold to the company by the Osborne family in 1973 when they acquired Bodegas Montecillo above. In 1999, having named the estate and designed the label to correspond with the pebbley earth found in the vineyard, a stylish new bodega was built for the relaunch of this utterly delicious single-vineyard wine. Finally Bodegas Lan makes a range of wines which epitomizes the best of everything Rioja has to offer. Its traditional blends are all good, representative examples of the region, whilst the top wines are sensational and show the concentrated structure and power that Rioja is sometimes capable of.

The route at this point drops down to Navarrete and Bodegas Bretón before continuing east to Logroño. Marqués de Murrieta sits by the side of the old road from Logroño to Zaragoza, 5km (3 miles) from the city centre (ring for directions as it can be tricky to find). The winery is housed in the grand 19th-century sandstone castle of Ygay, and a museum has recently been created to celebrate the history of the estate. In this particular range tradition mingles harmoniously with innovation, and if you're a fan of white Rioja then it doesn't come any better than the single-vineyard Capellanía Gran Reserva. For a more modern approach try Dalmau, which Murrieta considers to be a wine that marries tradition with innovation, though I find it very new wave and could easily have put it into my list of *alta expresión* wines on pp.65–6.

Two other wineries worth a visit near Logroño are Viña Ijalba and Juan Alcorta. Situated on the N111 road just north

BODEGAS IN RIOJA (CONTINUED)
. . . .

CVNE [B1]
Barrio de la Estación
26200 Haro
Tel: +34 941 304 800
www.cvne.com

Dinastía Vivanco [B2]
Ctra Nacional 232
26330 Briones
Tel: +34 941 322 332
www.dinastiavivanco.com

Finca Allende [B2]
Plaza Ibarra 1, 26330 Briones
Tel: +34 941 322 301
www.finca-allende.com

These four are all in Haro:-
López de Heredia [B1]
Tel: +34 941 310 244
www.lopezdeheredia.com
Muga [B1]
Tel: +34 941 311 825
www.bodegasmuga.com
La Rioja Alta [B1]
Tel: +34 941 310 346
www.riojalta.com
Roda [B1]
Tel: +34 941 303 001
www.roda.es

Route Three
Bodegas Lan [B3]
Paraje de Buicio
26360 Fuenmayor
Tel: +34 941 450 950
www.bodegaslan.com

Bretón [A/B3]
Ctra Fuenmayor – 1.5km
26370 Navarrete
Tel: +34 941 440 840
www.bodegasbreton.com

Finca Valpiedra [B3]
26360 Fuenmayor
Tel: +34 941 450 876
www.martinezbujanda.com

Juan Alcorta [B4]
Camino de Lapuebla 50
26006 Logroño
Tel: +34 941 279 900
www.bodegasjuanalcorta.com

continued on p.73

ABOVE *Underground tunnels at Viña Pomal, just outside Haro.*

BELOW *When you've had your fill of sniffing and slurping, why not indulge in some fine art at the museum of Rioja in Logroño (it has been closed for extensive renovations, so check it has re-opened before you visit).*

of the city, Ijalba is most noteworthy for having been the first organically certified estate in Rioja (1994). The vines are planted on abandoned opencast mines and the whole winemaking process, right down to the use of ecological tin capsules on the bottles, is carried out in an environmentally friendly way. When the Ijalba Graciano was launched in 1995 it was apparently the first such varietal wine in Rioja – it's highly individual and definitely worth trying. Juan Alcorta is part of the same group as Ysios and the bodega is equally lavish, although not as aesthetically beautiful.

Marqués, Museo, and Mercado

The city of Logroño is at the beating heart of Rioja and I'd suggest you stay right in the centre at the newly renovated Hotel Marqués de Vallejo. From here it's a quick stroll to the city's numerous bars, cafés, and restaurants, as well as the local museum and the daily food market. Open Monday–Friday 7.30am–1.30pm and 4–7.30pm, and Saturday mornings, the Mercado de Abastos is a wonderful place to stock up on cheap *chorizo*, cheeses, and all manner of Spanish delicacies.

Route Four: Rioja Baja

The final route heads east into an area known as Rioja Baja, a comparatively hot part of the region that's traditionally been associated with rosé wine – not surprising when you consider its next-door neighbour is Navarra. However, just as Navarra has recently proved itself capable of producing far more than basic pink plonk (good as that pink plonk may be), the Riojan side of the fence has also thrown up some surprises of late.

The route begins 30km (18.5 miles) east of Logroño at Barón de Ley. Although the website says that visits are not permitted here, when I was there the young team assured me they'd do their level best to accommodate anyone who telephoned in advance. The estate has a beautifully renovated and perfectly maintained 15th-century Benedictine monastery, complete with fully furnished bedrooms that are sadly never used. The top wine (and the best), Finca Monasteria, is not a *reserva* or *gran reserva*, rather it's what would be described as a true "modern" Rioja, with its dense dark colour and richly concentrated fruit.

The route winds its way east to Lodosa and then drops down to below the A68 motorway and Pradejón. Here Bodegas

Valsacro is run by the Escudero brothers who took over from their father and founder of the bodega, Benito Escudero. A new winery is currently being built and ambitious plans are afoot. From here cross back over the motorway and head northeast to San Adrián. Luis Gurpegui Muga was founded in 1872 and currently makes wines in Rioja, Navarra, and, like Bodegas Guelbenzu (see Navarra chapter, p.76), in Chile's Colchagua Valley. The wines from the estate in San Adrián are all red, under the Primi and Dominio de la Plana labels.

There are just two more bodegas on this route and the first is Viña Herminia in Aldeanueva de Ebro. Created in 1998, this bodega is producing some very good wines under the watchful eye of an Australian consultant. You can find out about visits (which include a tasting and the chance to buy wine) by logging onto www.larioja.org/turismo. Alfaro is the last stop on the route and the bodega is Palacios Remondo. This is the family estate on which Alvaro Palacios (see Priorat chapter, p.104) spent his formative years. With Alvaro's recent return as winemaker, his skill and characteristic vitality have breathed new life into the company. Its current flagship wine, Propiedad, shows what modern Riojan winemaking is all about.

Dinastía Vivanco

Just outside Briones is the newest and surely the most impressive wine museum in the world, Dinastía Vivanco. As you ascend the long incline towards the building's space-age sandy brick façade, a huge sculpted hand of black grapes proffers a grand, yet warm welcome into the light and airy entrance space. Opened in June 2004 by King Juan Carlos, the museum is arranged over three floors and has a garden containing 250 different varieties of vines. The 6-euro entrance fee includes a five-minute video and a tasting "with an expert" of Dinastía Vivanco crianza red. You'll need to allow around two hours for a visit and audio headsets in English are available. The extraordinary collection of artefacts took owner Pedro Vivanco 40 years to amass and includes works of art by Picasso, a 1300 BC rhyton (drinking horn), and over 3,500 corkscrews.

If you'd like to eat before the tour, there's also a restaurant, tucked discreetly behind the shop and coffee bar, that serves food far removed from the usual offerings found in most museum eateries. Lunching here in elegant cream and chocolate brown surroundings, overlooking a sweeping vista of vineyards, is a treat not to be missed. The bodega at Dinastía Vivanco makes two wines, a crianza and a reserva, both of which are highly drinkable, though the added age of the reserva gives it a silkier texture and a little more perfume. A white wine is produced, but it's sold only in the restaurant and, as Rafael Vivanco (son of Pedro) says, "It's for people who don't like red wine."

BODEGAS IN RIOJA (CONTINUED)

Marqués de Cáceres [B2]
Ctra de Logroño
26350 Cenicero
Tel: +34 941 455 064
www.marquesdecaceres.com

Marqués de Murrieta [B4]
Ctra Logroño – Zaragoza
5km, Apartado 109,
26080 Logroño
Tel: +34 941 271 370
www.marquesdemurrieta.com

Montecillo [A/B3]
Ctra Fuenmayor –
Navarrete 3km
26360 Fuenmayor
Tel: +34 941 440 125
www.osborne.es

Viña Ijalba [B4]
Ctra de Pamplona 1km
26006 Logroño
Tel: +34 941 261 100
www.ijalba.com

Route Four
Barón de Ley [B6]
Ctra Mendavia – Lodosa 5km
31587 Mendavia
Tel: +34 948 694 303
www.barondeley.com

Luis Gurpegui Muga [B8]
Avda Celso Muerza 8
31570 San Adrián
Tel: +34 948 670 050
www.gurpegui.es

Palacios Remondo [A10]
Ctra de Zaragoza 8
26540 Alfaro
Tel: +34 941 180 207
www.vinos
herenciaremondo.com

Valsacro [B7]
Ctra N 232
26510 Pradejón
Tel: +34 941 398 008
www.valsacro.com

Viña Herminia [A9]
La Vendimia 1
26559 Aldeanueva de Ebro
Tel: +34 941 144 169
www.vherminia.es

Navarra

Navarra sits cheek by jowl with Rioja, sharing much the same climate and landscape, yet it has undeservedly lived in the winemaking shadow of its more famous neighbour for centuries. As well as vines, wines, and bodegas galore, Navarra's countryside is strewn with beautiful monasteries and churches, thanks to the fact that the two pilgrims' routes meet here, at Puente la Reina. And if all that isn't enough to send you rushing to pack your bags, consider its golden fields, lush green pasture land, and delicious fresh produce.

An independent spirit

The citizens of Navarra are proud and protective of their independence. For centuries they've clung onto their unique standing, reinforced in the 1978 Spanish Constitution, as a "*communidad foral*" or chartered community with its own "*feuros*" or autonomous rights, originally bestowed by King Ferdinand in 1512. The people insist they are Navarrese and not Basque, but historical links with the Basque Country have led to the same independence of spirit, as well as culinary and cultural influences which are still in evidence today.

RIGHT *Demi-johns of old-vine Muscat are aged on the roof at Camilo Castilla.*

BELOW *Grapes in the stone-work at Santa María church in Olite.*

Navarra versus Rioja

If Rioja's winemaking is all about tradition, with strict rules and regulations intended to uphold and maintain its established practices, then Navarra's is about innovation, with far more freedom to flex its winemaking muscles and push formerly accepted boundaries to their limits. At least, that was how the situation appeared towards the end of the last century when a small revolution was taking place in Navarra.

The customary rosé for which the region had long been known started to be usurped by modern wines made from popular international varieties such as Chardonnay, Merlot, and Cabernet Sauvignon. This was all well and good, but what about the true flavours of Navarra? Where were they? And was it such a good idea to desert trusty old Garnacha which had kept the region in the pink for so long?

Things have moved on quite a lot from those early days of change. As Rioja looks to new winemaking technologies and begins to produce its "high expression" wines with modern fruit flavours, creamy new oak, and the occasional splash of Cabernet

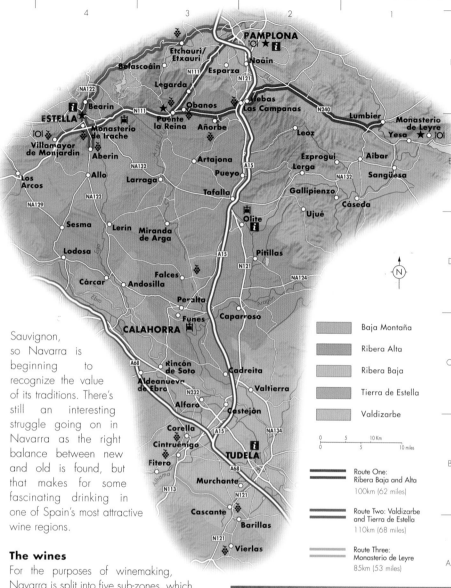

Sauvignon, so Navarra is beginning to recognize the value of its traditions. There's still an interesting struggle going on in Navarra as the right balance between new and old is found, but that makes for some fascinating drinking in one of Spain's most attractive wine regions.

The wines

For the purposes of winemaking, Navarra is split into five sub-zones, which are important for their climatic differences. Put simply, the south of the region is warmer and drier, whilst the further north you go the cooler and wetter it gets as the landscape becomes more mountainous and the influence of the sea is more keenly felt. Red grape varieties naturally flourish in the centre of the region, whilst the whites, especially Chardonnay, prefer the higher ground.

To understand the sub-zones, think of the region as a giant "T" shape. The first three of the five sub-zones, which run from west to east

BODEGAS IN NAVARRA
. . . .

Alzania [E5]
Cardiel 1
31210 Los Arcos
Tel: +34 639 078 782
alzania@knet.es

Camilo Castilla [B3]
Santa Bárbara 40
31591 Corella
Tel: +34 948 781 021
www.bodegascamilo
castilla.com

Castillo de Monjardín [E4]
Viña Rellanada s/n
31242 Villamayor
de Monjardín
Tel: +34 948 537 412
www.monjardin.es
**Tours 11am–1.30pm Sat,
1 hour including tasting.**

Guelbenzu [B2/3]
San Juan 14
31520 Cascante
Tel: +34 948 850 055
www.guelbenzu.com

Inurrieta [D3]
Ctra Falces –
Miranda de Arga 30km,
31370 Falces
Tel: +34 948 737 309
www.bodegainurrieta.com

**Irache and the Monasterio
[E4]** Monasterio de Irache 1
31240 Ayegui
Tel: +34 948 551 932
irache@irache.com
www.bodegasirache.es

Julián Chivite [B3]
Ribera 34
ES-31592 Cintruénigo
Tel: +34 948 811 000
www.chivite.com
**Visits 9am–6pm Mon–Fri.
Ring for an appointment.**

La Lombana [A2/3]
50513 Vierlas, Aragón
Tel: +34 976 191 000

continued on p.79

along the horizontal crossbar are Tierra de Estella, Valdizarbe, and Baja Montaña. Ribera Baja is at the bottom of the vertical stem of the T, and Ribera Alta sits on top of it. Of the three suggested routes below, Route One covers the two Riberas to the south, Route Two is mainly Tierra de Estella and the eastern side of Valdizarbe, and Route Three heads east into Valdizarbe and Baja Montaña.

As already mentioned, until about 15 years ago Navarra was considered to be rosé country, with records from as far back as the 15th century making favourable reference to the region's "rosado". Even today you'll find most bodegas making a fruity, quaffable, good-value rosado from Garnacha grapes. However, the rest of the range will usually be made from international varieties and Tempranillo, in a relatively modern and appealing style, quite different to that of their neighbour's, yet with an increasingly traditional touch. As the wines are far less well known than those of Rioja, they tend to be great value, so I'd suggest you stock up whilst you can.

Technology in Navarra
You can't begin to appreciate the developments and advances that Navarra has made in recent years without knowing a little about Evena (Estación de Viticultura y Enología de Navarra). Situated just outside Olite, this is the Navarra government's Oenological Station and it's here that pioneering research is undertaken, analytical tests are carried out, advice and training are offered to winemakers, and an experimental vineyard and bodega are monitored. Evena is not unique, but it was one of the first of its kind and is very highly regarded in the wine world today. You'll find it just north of Olite if you want to take a look.

Getting there
Although you may prefer somewhere smaller and quieter, Pamplona is the region's capital and it's a great place to base yourself. Not only does it have a stunning Gothic cathedral, a very good museum, a ruined citadel, and the famous Plaza de Toros (bullring), there's also an early morning market to visit, a maze of tiny old streets through which to wander, plenty of good hotels, and some of the region's best restaurants and bars.

The closest major airport is Bilbao, 160km (100 miles) northwest of the city. If you want to fly to Pamplona itself, however, it does have an airport (tel: +34 948 168 750, www.aena.es) and there are flights from both Barcelona (480km/298 miles to the east) and Madrid (407km/252 miles south). The train station is to the north of the town on Avenida San Jorge and can be reached by catching the No 9

bus from Paseo de Sarasate. Trains (www.renfe.es) run directly to Pamplona from Barcelona, Madrid, and San Sebastián, but if you're travelling from Bilbao you'll need to go via Burgos, as there's no direct route.

ABOVE *Driving between wineries can be just as spectacular as some of the wines you'll taste.*

The bus station is on Calle Conde Oliveto, just in front of the citadel, and although you could use local buses to tour the region, they are limiting in terms of the countryside they cover.

If arriving by car from Bilbao then head south from the city down the A68/E80 motorway and take the turning off towards Vitoria-Gasteiz at junction 5. At junction 352 head east towards Pamplona on the N1. This road becomes the N240A before you take the A15 down to Pamplona. For car hire, *see* www.carhireexpress.co.uk.

Travelling around

There's a lot of scope for wine-lovers in Navarra, so here are three suggested itineraries for the area.

Route One summary This route covers the area directly south of Pamplona, beginning in a tiny village called Vierlas. It then works its way north via Cascante, Cintruénigo, and on to Corella. Moving out of the Ribera Baja zone and into the Ribera Alta, the route then continues on up to Falces and finishes in the beautiful little town of Olite. This route is approximately 100km (62 miles).

WHERE TO EAT

Bodegón Sarría [F2/3]
Calle de la Estafeta 50
31001 Pamplona
Tel: +34 948 227 713

Europa [F2/3]
Espoz y Mina 11
31001 Pamplona
Tel: +34 948 221 800
europa@heuropa.com

Rodero [F2/3]
C/Emilio Arrieta 3
31002 Pamplona
Tel: +34 948 228 035
info@restauranterodero.com
www.restauranterodero.com

BELOW *Electricity-generating windmills are a familiar feature of Navarra's landscape.*

Route Two summary This route concentrates on an area to the west of Pamplona. Beginning in the city itself the route firstly heads southwest to the town of Puente la Reina before continuing to Villamayor de Monjardín. You then double back on yourself and drop down to Aberin before heading north through Estella, via the Monasterio de Irache, and finally northeast back into Pamplona. This route is approximately 110km (68 miles).

Route Three summary The final route goes southwest of Pamplona and then east, and although there are fewer bodegas en route, its culmination at the breathtaking Monasterio de Leyre makes the trip more than worthwhile. The route is approximately 85km (53 miles) and goes from Pamplona to Obanos, then works its way east via Las Campanas/Tiebas, and along the main N240 to the monastery.

Route One: Ribera Baja and Alta
Bodegas Guelbenzu is a great place to visit as it offers the contrast of an extremely old winery in Cascante (rather like a lacy pink wedding cake) with an ultra modern building out in Vierlas – which is where the route starts. On a clear day from the "lookout tower" at the Vierlas winery you can see Rioja, Navarra, Campo de Borja, and the mountains of Ribera del

Duero. The vineyards run along an old railway line which is good to walk or cycle along. When you make an appointment, ask for directions to the Vierlas winery as it's a little tricky to find. This forward-thinking company prefers the simplicity of colourful labels to terms such as "*crianza*" and "*reserva*". (These terms may guarantee a minimum period of ageing, but are no real indicator as to the quality of the wine in the bottle, as bad wine can be aged for as long as good and it will still be poor wine. So it's important to get to know which producers you like and can trust, rather than always relying on these terms.) If you're looking for value for money, the Guelbenzu Vierlas 2003, with its sunny yellow label and warm, spicy, blackberry fruit, is hard to beat.

From Cascante take the NA6900 west to Cintruénigo where you'll find Bodegas Julián Chivite. This impressive company is Navarra's top wine exporter and owns two wineries in Navarra and one in Rioja. The Cintruénigo bodega is the original, established in 1647 and now in the eleventh generation of family ownership. Visits are easy to arrange and the Gran Feudo wines are a very reliable buy – especially good are the Garnacha rosé and the Viñas Viejas red blend.

Sweet talking

Just up the NA160 in the centre of Corella, a bright yellow, flower-clad courtyard welcomes you to Camilo Castilla, one of the loveliest bodegas imaginable. Sweet wines made from old Muscat are the speciality here and the historic barrel room smells just like spicy Christmas cake. This is one of the only wineries in Spain where you'll find dessert wines being aged in demi-johns on an open flat roof, and for this sight alone it's worth a visit (*see p.76*). If you like sweet wine, or even if you think you don't, then you must buy at least one bottle of Capricho de Goya (a half bottle at the winery is just over 5 euros) – it's indescribably good.

New face in Falces

The route now heads north up the back roads and winds its way to Inurrieta, just outside Falces. The directions are tricky so I'll try to make them as detailed as possible. Head north on the LR285 for 9km (5.5 miles), then left onto the N232 for 1km (0.6 miles) towards Rincón de Soto. Turn right into Carretera de Alfaro, then right onto the LR115, which becomes the NA115, and continue on this for around 20km (12.4 miles). On the way you might want to stop off near Funes where you'll find a Roman wine vat dating from the second century AD. Turn right onto the NA660. At the roundabout take the fourth exit onto the NA 6600, then left onto the NA6100 straight up to the winery, which is situated between Falces and Miranda de Arga. And by the time you get there you'll need a drink!

BODEGAS IN NAVARRA (CONTINUED)

Nekeas [E3]
C/Las Huertas s/n
31154 Añorbe
Tel: +34 948 350 296
nekeas@nekeas.com
www.nekeas.com
Shop open 9am–2pm Mon–Fri, 4–6pm Sat.

Ochoa [D2/3]
Alcalde Maillata 2
31390 Olite
Tel: +34 948 740 006
info@bodegasochoa.com
www.bodegasochoa.com

Orvalaiz [E/F3]
Ctra Pamplona –
Logroño s/n
31151 Obanos
Tel: +34 948 344 437
bodega@orvalaiz.es

Señorío de Arínzano [E4]
Aberin
31240 Estella
Tel: +34 948 555 285
Visits are restricted so make sure you check first.

Señorío de Otazu [F3]
Gabarbide SA
31174 Echauri
Tel: +34 948 329 200
export@otazu.com
www.otazu.com

Señorío de Sarría [F3]
Avda de Pío X11 31 Bajo
31008 Pamplona
Tel: +34 948 198 540
info@bodesa.net
www.bodegadesarria.com

Valcarlos [E5]
Ctra Circunvalacion s/n
31210 Los Arcos
Tel: +34 948 640 806

Vinícola Navarra [F2/3]
Ctra de Zaragoza 14km
31398 Muruarte de Reta
Tel: +34 902 239 767
info@byb.es
www.byb.es

ABOVE *Guelbenzu winery in Cascante was built in 1851 by the family's great-grandfather.*

Inurrieta is a brand new operation which planted its first vines in 1999. It's a friendly family business and they'll be happy to arrange a tour to suit you, which can then be followed by lunch amongst the vines. (If you do plan to have lunch here you may decide to do the route in reverse, beginning with a night in Olite, and then zooming straight back up the main motorway to Pamplona when you've finished.)

Sleeping in a castle
From here it's a short trip to the delightful old town of Olite, where the state-run *parador* in the centre of the town is the place to stay. It's a medieval castle built in the early 1500s by King Carlos III of Navarra. The building was restored in 1940 and it sits on the main *plaza* next to the church of Santa María. Look closely at the elaborate Gothic façade of the latter and you'll see that grapes have been a part of people's lives here for generations. One extremely good winery in the area which doesn't allow visits is Ochoa. However, if you want to buy its wines you'll find them in the old winery in the town centre, which now houses a shop (see p.79).

Route Two: Valdizarbe and Tierra de Estella
This route, which begins in Pamplona, follows the Pilgrims' Route towards Santiago and is packed with historical gems, including monasteries and Roman hermitages. The first artefact you'll come across, however, is in Puente la Reina, and it's the medieval bridge after which the town is named.

The extraordinarily beautiful Señorío de Sarría estate (there's a map with directions at www.bodegadesarria.com) has its very own on-site chapel and lies 8km (5 miles) north of the town. The most recent innovation here is the Viñedos range of six single-variety wines. When Jesús Lezaun became winemaker in 2001 he was looking to create a more modern style of wine with less barrel-ageing, fresher fruit flavours, and better structure. The most interesting to try is the Viñedos 7 made from 100% Graciano, a variety rarely bottled alone and normally hidden away in the blend of traditional red Rioja.

If you continue along in the pilgrims' footsteps you'll come to Villamayor de Monjardín and Castillo de Monjardín situated in the San Esteban valley. A well-equipped, modern winery using international varieties to make white, red, and rosé wines, this is also a good place to stop for lunch, as it has an on-site restaurant (for restaurant bookings tel: +34 948 537 589).

Drive back towards Pamplona and then drop down to Aberin on the NA122, to Señorío de Arínzano. In the 1980s Chivite spread its wings from its original bodega in the south (see Route One) to the west of Navarra, and began this single-estate project. The renowned Navarrese architect, Rafael Moneo, was given the difficult task of creating a modern "winery built for wine", whilst at the same time respecting the three existing old buildings, the surrounding oak and poplar trees, and the river Ega running quietly through. It's a wonderful achievement and a fitting building in which to produce the consistently impressive Chivite Colección 125.

The sacred heart of Tierra de Estella

As you drive north towards Estella, stop off at the Benedictine Monasterio de Irache, which was founded either by the Visigoths sometime between the 5th and 8th centuries, or by San Veremundo in the 10th, depending on which source you choose to believe. What is certain is that it became a Pilgrims' hospice in the 11th century and since 1891 has also had its own wine bodega, today producing a wide range of traditional-tasting wines. Although there's a small shop/ museum, what you must seek out is the drinking fountain which offers complimentary water and wine to weary pilgrims en route to Santiago de Compostela.

Estella is the main hub of the area and the town dates from the 12th century. It was an early trading centre and people have been buying and selling their wares here at the Thursday market since the 15th century. If you have the time, Estella is also home to quite a few of those historical gems I was talking about earlier. They come in the form of churches, such as that of San Pedro de la Rúa with its Romanesque cloister, as well as palaces and beautiful old manor houses.

From Estella pick up the NA120 heading north and then head east by taking a right onto the NA7000 and then a left onto the NA700, which will take you all the way to Echauri and Señorío de Otazu. This winery claims to own the most northerly red wine vineyards in Spain, just 58km (36 miles) from the Atlantic. Look out for the concrete ceiling in the Hollywood-style barrel cellar, which at enormous cost has been made to look like wood. All the grapes come from the estate and although you may not be offered a tasting of the top-of-the-range Altar, the visit and tasting are free, and all wines are available to buy at the bodega.

Dinner time

If you want to treat yourself to an amazing dinner in Navarra, then book a table at Rodero (www.restauranterodero.com), just opposite the famous bullring in the centre of Pamplona. Here the eight-course *degustación* menu includes such delights as Cuajada de Coco y Moluscos. Served in a Martini glass, it's a kind of creamy coconut mousse studded with bright orange trout eggs over which your waiter will carefully pour a warm cream

BELOW *This little boy with grapes in hand adds decoration to the delightful yellow courtyard at Camilo Castilla.*

NAVARRA'S DO

....

**Consejo Regulador
Denominación de
Origen Navarra**
Rua Romana s/n
31390 Olite
Tel: +34 948 741 812
consejoregulador@
vinonavarra.com
www.vinonavarra.com

RIGHT *The annual October pepper market is held in Puente la Reina.*

BELOW *The Monasterio de Irache offers complimentary wine and water to weary pilgrims on their journey to Santiago de Compostela.*

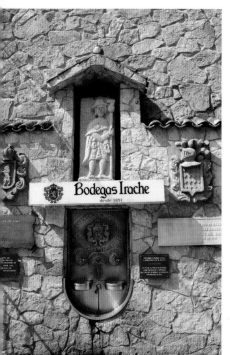

of sea urchin. You may also be offered a warm terrine of pig confit with chunks of caramelized apple and hazelnuts, sweet and sour *jus*, and a topping of crispy pork skin. The menu includes a couple of melt-in-the mouth desserts and is rounded off with coffee and a teaspoon of dark chocolate truffle mousse. At around 60 euros, it's a steal.

Route Three: Monasterio de Leyre
Head southwest out of Pamplona on the N 111 and then pick up the left turning to Obanos (N111a/NA6061). Orvalaiz produces some of the best-value rosé I've come across in Spain and here's your chance to stock up. This is a co-op and although it's not the most exciting place to visit, if you drop by in October you may just see the vats of bright pink rosé must, bubbling and gurgling as it gushes along towards the fermentation tanks. Winemaker Kepa Sagastizabal makes an Orvalaiz Cabernet Sauvignon rosé especially for the export market (2.55 euros in the winery shop), which is slightly drier than, and interesting to compare with, the Tempranillo/Garnacha blend reserved for the domestic market.

Top-notch Navarra
If you take the NA601 east and then drop down on the NA6013 you'll find Añorbe, a wonderfully traditional Navarrese village, complete with little old leather-faced ladies in wrinkled stockings carrying large loaves of fresh, crusty bread. Not only is this a delightful place for a quiet afternoon's stroll, it's also the location of one of the best wineries in Navarra. Nekeas sits on the outskirts of Añorbe and was the brainchild of eight local families who had the vision to create this cooperative estate back in 1989. The winery was built in 1993 and has been producing increasingly good wine ever since. The Rhône-style "El Chaparral" is one of the best of a very exciting range, and if you want a bargain then stock up on the Nekeas Joven Tempranillo.

Pilgrims' rest
The company that owns Vinícola Navarra claims that it was the first cellar to be established in the region back in 1864, and as I wasn't around at the time, I'm going to take its word for it. It seems to like firsts, having apparently also bottled the first wine almost 100 years later. Today the bodega is owned by the giant Bodegas y

Bebidas group and it's a thriving company producing seven million bottles of wine per year. The local town of Las Campanas is on the Pilgrims' Route to Santiago, and an interesting nod to the estate's past lies in the tasting room which was once a hospital for sick travellers.

The place is a bit old-fashioned and I found my visit here a little bit uninspiring, but it was a drizzly, dull day, so maybe my enthusiasm was dampened by that. The upside was that the wines were actually surprisingly decent, and certainly very good value for money.

Magnificent monastery

From Vinícola Navarra just follow the road east until you reach the Monasterio de Leyre. There are lots of interesting detours to be made en route with the towns of Sangüesa, Gallipienzo, Aibar, Cáseda, and Ujué all boasting ancient churches and some wonderful views of the Aragón River valley. The monastery itself sits on a hillside which offers a spectacular panorama of the surrounding countryside, with the deep aquamarine reservoir of Yesa at its centre. Here you can book yourself in for the night, visit the Romanesque crypt, listen to Gregorian chanting, eat good honest food in the large refectory-style restaurant, sink a few glasses of Navarra *vino tinto*, and then fall into bed for a peaceful night's sleep.

If you decide to continue on to Somontano, the drive is absolutely spectacular as you drop down off the N240 and onto the A132 towards Huesca. The rugged slate-grey and terracotta cliff faces, thick with fragrant pine, towering over the deep green waters of the Río Gállego beneath, are quite simply breathtaking.

Seeing red

It's almost impossible to visit Navarra without hearing, reading, or seeing something to do with its most famous festival, that of San Fermin. From July 6 to 14 each year people are either uncontrollably drawn to, or determinedly avoid at all costs, the city of Pamplona and its bullfighting festival. The fame of the

USEFUL INFORMATION

Asociación Bodegas de Navarra
Apartado de Correos 316
General Chinchilla 4
31002 Pamplona
Tel: +34 948 077 071
www.vinonavarra.com

Estella Tourist Office
San Nicolás 1,
31200 Estella
Tel: +34 948 556 301
oit.estella@cfnavarra.es

Olite Tourist Office
Rua Major 1 Bajo
31390 Olite
Tel: +34 948 741 703
oit.olite@cfnavarra.es

Pamplona Tourist Office
Eslava 1
(Cnr Plaza S Francisco)
31001 Pamplona
Tel: +34 948 206 540
oit.pamplona@cfnavarra.es

Tudela Tourist Office
Plaza Vieja 1
31500 Tudela
Tel: +34 948 848 058
oit.tudela@cfnavarra.es

ABOVE *The entrance to the Parador de Olite in the main Plaza Teobaldos.*

festival was perpetuated after the publication of Ernest Hemingway's novel *The Sun Also Rises*. During the festivities you could stay in the same hotel as the novelist, the one-star La Perla (tel: +34 948 227 706), although if you were hoping to sleep in the same bed, you'll have a long wait, as it's reputedly booked for the next 40 years.

The most bizarre feature of the nine-day, non-stop partying is the tradition of bull running. Every morning at 8am the bulls pegged for fighting that day are let loose to run through the streets in hot pursuit of their young challengers. To save any nasty slip-ups the authorities in Pamplona sprayed the streets with a type of anti-skid solution for the first time last year, which may have lessened the thrill of the chase, but at least, one assumes, they all turned up for the fight.

If all this is far too much for you and all you want is some good *jamón* and a glass of red wine, then Bodegón Sarría (Calle de la Estafeta 50) is central, lively, and has a nice authentic feel to it.

Peppered up
The only thing which links Navarra's two most compelling products is the colour red. But don't be put off, their colour is the only fiery element of Pimientos de Piquillo once their firm flesh has been roasted into soft, sweet submission. The Navarrese think so highly of these peppers that they've given them their own appellation "Pimientos Piquillo de Lodosa", and, whether you eat them freshly roasted from Puente la Reina's annual October market, or from the tin you carried them home in, the flavour is fantastic.

Finally, some facts and figures
In 2004, Navarra's 120 bodegas produced a total of just over 87 million litres of wine (the equivalent of 116 million bottles), with around two-thirds of that coming from the cooperatives. The total vineyard area in Navarra stood at 17,927 hectares. In terms of kilos of grapes produced, Tempranillo yielded the highest quantity at 54,270,553 kilos, closely followed by Garnacha at 43,329,807. Next came Cabernet Sauvignon and Merlot which were almost neck and neck, though some way behind the other two at just over 18 million each. For whites, Viura and Chardonnay were produced in the largest quantities, though white wines accounted for only 5% of the total bottles produced in Navarra in 2004. The majority of the wine made in the region was red, a trend which has been slowly gaining ground over the past decade. In 1990, 64% of total wine production was red and 31% was rosé. But by 2004 rosé had dropped to 22%, with red up to 73%.

Somontano

S omontano could hardly be described as the easiest place to get to. It's slap bang in the middle between Bilbao and Barcelona, around 300km (186 miles) from either airport. It has no golden sandy beaches, no world-famous chefs, and certainly no great reputation for producing wine – or so you might think. But if you decided, perfectly reasonably, to ignore it and visit instead one of its better-known, more accessible neighbours, you'd be missing an absolute treat.

A little revolution

Somontano, which means "at the foot of the mountains", sits quietly in the shadow of the Pyrenees to the north and the Sierras de Guara and Salinas a little closer to home. It's a compact place given over to ancient villages, rocky river gorges, and scattered mountainous scrub that at times make you wonder if you've wandered into cowboy country rather than anything to do with wine-growing. It is, however, a little-known fact that a small vinous revolution has taken place here over the past 20 or so years, and the fruits of this transformation are currently ripe for the drinking.

Aragón

The *autonomía* of Aragón consists of three provinces, with Huesca being the most northerly of the three, and the one which contains the sub-zone of Somontano. Aragón's place in history was assured during the 15th century when its prince, Ferdinand, married Isabella of Castile. This attachment shortly led to the joining of the old County of Castile, the Kingdom of Aragón, and the County of Catalonia under one royal house, and ultimately to the unification of Spain. But the production of wine in the region goes back much farther than that. It's believed that as early as the 2nd century BC the Romans brought vines to the region, along with some useful Italian winemaking know-how. During the Middle Ages the monasteries were largely responsible for the spread of vine cultivation throughout the entire province. Finally, the unwelcome arrival of the devastating bug phylloxera in France's vineyards during the 19th century meant that Aragón found its wines in greater demand than ever.

BELOW Bosque Hierro *or* Iron Wood *is a sculpture by one of Enate's local artists, Vicente García Plana.*

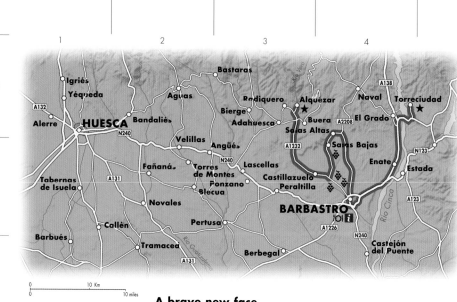

0 _____ 10 Km
0 _____ 10 miles

▰▰▰▰ Route: Alquézar
▰▰▰▰ to Torreciudad
80–90km (50–56 miles)

A brave new face

Somontano is a region perfectly placed to make top-quality wines. It has a continental climate, ready access to river water, well-drained, fertile soils, protection from surrounding mountain ranges, and exposure to the ripening sun. But throughout its history, Aragón as a whole simply didn't move with the winemaking times, and around 20 years ago things had virtually ground to a halt. In 1985 all that finally changed for Somontano, as the long-awaited DO (an incredible 11 years in the creating) was finally granted. From the time of the formation of the DO, Somontano was pegged as a new leading light in the modern Spanish wine revolution, and great things were forecast for this tiny region of around 4,000ha of vines and just 15 bodegas. An extraordinary amount has happened in a very short space of time, with something virtually being created from nothing, but although there's been huge investment and a pioneering will to succeed, has Somontano really delivered the unique and exciting wines expected of it? And if not, why not?

A sense of belonging...

If we compare Somontano to Priorat, we can perhaps begin to appreciate why Somontano hasn't made quite the big splash expected of it. Both are pocket-sized regions that have experienced recent winemaking revolutions. But there's a fundamental difference. When Priorat's revolutionaries took centre stage 15–20 years ago, the grapes were already there. They had old-vine, indigenous grape varieties to play with, planted in Priorat's special slate soil. What they did was to form them into wonderfully modern wines, but wines which had a unique character thanks to the age of the vines and the extraordinary ground in which they were planted. The problem for anyone wishing to buy these wines today is that they've reached virtual cult status, and as such, they're often prohibitively expensive.

The winemakers of Somontano on the other hand began with a completely blank slate – and on the positive side, had no outmoded DO regulations to hamper creativity – but in favouring international varieties, such as Chardonnay and Cabernet Sauvignon, they've so far had to forgo the creation of a true, recognizably distinct Somontano style. To be fair, international varieties do seem to work well here, and why shouldn't one of Spain's better regions dedicate itself to producing classic New World-style wines at an affordable price?

So to conclude, Somontano has changed beyond recognition in the space of two decades. It currently produces highly drinkable, well-made wines in a familiar style (that we like), at a price we can all afford. The only question is, could it be doing better with its given resources? What I hope is that in setting the current scene I've whetted your appetite and your curiosity to find out more, and it's now up to you to try the wines and draw your own conclusions.

Getting there

It's virtually impossible to contemplate touring Somontano without a car, as it's too small to have a decent public transport system. If you're hiring a car in Barcelona, because of the distances involved, I'd advise taking the main A2/E90 autoroute west to Lleida/Lérida and then picking up the N240 which goes straight to Barbastro. If you're approaching from Bilbao, begin by heading south and east on the A68/E05 as far as Zaragoza, where you'll need to pick up the N330/E7 to Huesca, and from there head east on the N240 to Barbastro. At Huesca you might like to take a slight detour and drive up to the stunning Monasterio de Leyre for a night (see p.81 for details). You can also take a train from Barcelona or Bilbao (though the service from the latter is limited) to Zaragoza (www.renfe.es), and hire a car here if you'd prefer a little less driving (www.carhireexpress.co.uk).

Travelling around

Route summary Head south from Alquézar down to just beyond Castillazuelo, then north up to Salas Bajas. You then loop back down to Barbastro and head out of the other end of town north up to Torreciudad, just beyond the little town of Enate. The route is around 80–90km (50–56 miles) and you may want to break it up by saving Torreciudad for a second day.

Route: Alquézar to Torreciudad

Alquézar, a beautiful old Pyrenean village, is a lovely place to spend a day or two before you embark on your wine tour – you may even decide to try your hand at a spot of canyoning (see

BODEGAS IN SOMONTANO

Blecua [B4]
Ctra Barbastro –
Naval 3.7km
22300 Barbastro
Huesca
Tel: +34 974 302 216
www.bodegablecua.com

Enate [B4]
Ctra de Barbastro
– Naval 9km
22314 Salas Bajas
Huesca
Tel: +34 974 302 580
www.enate.es

Lalanne [B4]
Torre de San Marcos
22300 Barbastro
Huesca
Tel: +34 974 310 689
blalanne@jazzfree.com

Osca [B3]
C/La Iglesia 1
22124 Ponzano
Huesca
Tel: +34 974 319 017/175
www.bodegasosca.com

Pirineos [B4]
Ctra Barbastro
– Naval 3.5km
22300 Barbastro
Huesca
Tel: +34 974 312 273
www.bodegapirineos.com

Sierra de Guara [B3]
Ctra de Abiego 0.2km
22124 Lascellas
Huesca
Tel: +34 974 319 363
www.bodega
ssierradeguara.es

Viñas del Vero [B4]
Finca de San Marcos
Ctra Barbastro
– Naval 3.7km
22300 Barbastro
Huesca
Tel: +34 974 302 216
www.vinasdelvero.es

ABOVE *Ancient trees bask in the Somontano sunshine.*

RIGHT *The hilltop village of Alquézar is a good place to begin your tour of Somontano.*

p.90) for which the area is famous. The village itself (as well as the hotel Villa de Alquézar, *see* box on right), sits atop a rocky hill and is dominated by the Colegiata de Santa María la Mayor, for which guided tours can be arranged (11am–1.30pm, 4.30–6/7.30pm). Alquézar gets busy in the summer, so if you'd prefer to stay somewhere a little quieter, the beautiful La Posada de Lalola, with just six rooms in nearby Buera (*see* right), may be a better option.

Near neighbours

Around 20km (12.4 miles) from Alquézar as you head south on the A1232 you'll come across two of Somontano's three major wineries, Viñas del Vero and Pirineos, sitting opposite each other, just by the side of the road.

Viñas del Vero, established in 1986, was the first pioneering bodega of the new DO. After beginning life in an experimental winery in Salas Bajas, the company now has an impressive new facility (inaugurated in 1993), complete with a smart shop for stocking up on wines and all manner of related objects. This hugely successful company owns over 1,000ha of vines and its wines are made predominantly from international varieties. You won't find rusticity and quirky local charm on a visit here, but you will see how clean, modern wine is made for consumers who've grown to expect New World-style reliability.

Close by is its flagship Bodegas Blecua, a château-style winery housed in a beautiful old 17th-century villa. Just one wine is produced here from the company's top seven vineyard plots. It's a premium blend of international and local varieties made in very limited quantities, so if you can afford to stash a bottle or two in the boot of your car I'd recommend you do so.

Pirineos was originally a co-op, but is now a private company with former members (now shareholders) providing most of its grapes. There's been huge investment since privatization in 1993 and the frequent use of indigenous varieties such as Macabeo, Moristel, and Parraleta makes tasting and buying wine here an absolute must for inquisitive enthusiasts.

Enate and the art of wine

If you now take the road north towards Salas Bajas in about 10km (6 miles) you'll come to Enate. This was established in 1991 and named after the location of the winery's first vineyard a few kilometres away. The owner of the bodega is an art fanatic and the stunning red brick exterior of the building leads you into a space in which art and wine share centre stage. As well as local sculptures and a huge, colourful picture made up of boxes depicting the story of wine, there's gallery space containing 170 works of art, many of which are original commissions for the Enate bottle labels – look out for the one by Antoni Tàpies, it's a

WHERE TO EAT
. . . .

El Cenador de San Julián [B4]
Avda de la Merced 64
22300 Barbastro, Huesca
Tel: +34 974 311 205

El Flor [B4]
C/Goya 3,
22300 Barbastro, Huesca
Tel: +34 974 315 079

El Puntillo [A3]
See the box opposite.

Frutería del Vero [B4]
22300 Barbastro, Huesca

favourite of mine. Enate is also very much involved with an artistic festival organized by the Somontano DO which is held each year in Barbastro during the first weekend in August (tel: +34 974 313 031). Ticket price includes *tapas* and a glass of wine. Enate invites singers such as Julio Iglesias to perform at the winery during the festival.

Enate receives over 15,000 visitors a year and could at first appear to be a little too slick an operation for those in search of the "real thing" in terms of a winery visit. However, don't be put off as the hour-and-a-half tour includes a properly informative video (as opposed to some of the ad campaigns you will, at times, be subjected to) plus a chance to experience the superb aroma room. There's also a free tasting of the wines, for which the grapes are grown in an environmentally friendly way.

In the shop you'll find wine videos, local meats and cheeses, olive oil and balsamic, and of course the wines. The whole range is impressive, but the Cabernet Sauvignon rosé, packed with juicy raspberry and red cherry fruit, is one of the best I've tasted in Spain – and perfect for a well-earned picnic in the sunshine.

Barbastro and Torreciudad

The route continues north on the A2208 for a short while before you loop back down south to Barbastro. The town itself is a pleasant enough place and sitting, as I've been fortunate enough to do, in the Plaza de Mercado on a balmy Sunday evening, watching the older generation amble by on their *paseo* whilst the

WHERE TO STAY

Gran Hotel Ciudad de Barbastro [B4]
Plaza de Mercado 4
22300 Barbastro, Huesca
Tel: +34 974 308 900
www.ghbarbastro.com
€72 (double room)

El Puntillo [A3]
C/Iglesia 4
22147 Adahuesca
Tel: +34 974 318 168
www.elpuntillo.com
€40–50 (double room)
€63–78 (apartment)

La Posada de Lalola [A3]
Buera, 22146 Huesca
Tel: +34 974 318 437
www.laposadadelalola.com
€78 (double room)

Villa de Alquézar [A3]
C/Pedro Arnal Cavero 12
22145 Alquézar, Huesca
Tel: +34 974 318 416
www.villadealquezar.com
€35–51 (double room)

USEFUL INFORMATION

Turismo Conjunto de San Julián y Santa Lucía
Avda de la Merced 64
22300 Barbastro, Huesca
Tel: +34 974 308 350
www.barbastro-ayto.es

Websites to visit:
www.alquezar.org – the
actividades link will give
you canyoning information.
www.barranque.com/map
a-barbastro/index2.htm
www.dosomontano.com
www.radiquero.com/alque
zar/ – for information
on the Colegiata.
www.torreciudad.org

RIGHT *The beauty of this* santuari
*in Montferri, Tarragona, speaks
for itself.*

BELOW *The austere HQ of Opus
Dei is worth a short detour if
you're a Dan Brown fan.*

youngsters play tag in their Sunday best, makes you feel you've discovered what rural Spain is really about. I was sitting, as it happens, outside the Gran Hotel Ciudad (see p.89), which is about as far from "rural" as it's possible to imagine, and none the worse for that. It's a stylish modern hotel offering state-of-the-art accommodation and food, for which it asks attractively modest prices. To the southwest of the town you'll also find, situated behind the bullring, the restored Conjunto de San Julián y Santa Lucía, which houses the tourist office, the headquarters of the DO Somontano, a wine museum, and a restaurant.

From Barbastro take the N123 up to Torreciudad. For anyone who's read *The Da Vinci Code* then the 25km (15.5-mile) trip is a must. In Torreciudad you'll find the headquarters, built in 1975, of the ultra-Catholic Opus Dei movement (www.opusdei.org) in all its sinister red brick glory. The most impressive sight though, is the breathtaking view over the aquamarine El Grado reservoir at the top. All the way up from Barbastro the countryside is stunning and a lazy picnic en route might be just the ticket after all that tasting.

Canyoning

I'm not totally convinced that if you're reading this book you're the canyoning type, but if you feel the urge to have a go then you're in one of the best places in Europe to try it. North of the road between Barbastro and Huesca lies the Sierra de Guara, where the canyons of the Río Vero and various other rivers provide the perfect setting for such crazy antics. Alquézar is the hub of activities with places offering guided canyoning trips (*descenso de barrancos*) to suit all tastes. It will cost 50–60 euros per person.

Valle de Cinca (Huesca)

If you'd like to visit at a nascent wine area, south of Somontano in the Río Cinca valley you'll find the Valle del Cinca. At present the winery most worthy of a mention belongs to the Codorníu group. Established in 2001 and named Nuviana (www.nuviana.com), it's located on the San Miguel estate, which forms part of the denomination Vinos de la Tierra del Valle del Cinca. It's located 11km (6.8 miles) along the A1241 (off the A1234 as you head south). This state-of-the-art winery has six separate estates providing it with mainly international grapes. The name Nuviana is derived from an old Spanish word "novellana", meaning a clutch of newborn chicks – appropriate, as the estate is an important sanctuary for migrating birds and an area of outstanding ecological interest.

Catalonia

. . . .

Catalonia – all of the regions from here to the end of the book fall within the *autonomía* of Catalonia. So before we head off into the delightfully varied landscapes and wines of Spain's northeast corner, here's a brief look at this unique area.

First things first

The Catalans, perhaps more so than the Navarrese or even the Basques, have shown an extraordinary independence of spirit throughout their long history. So much so that Catalonia today often seems more like a separate little country squeezed between France and Spain, than merely one of Spain's self-governing *autonomías*. It has its own language, culture, and cuisine, the latter of which proudly competes with the Basque Country's for pre-eminence in Spain. Note: "Catalonia" is the English word for the region. In Castilian it is "Cataluña" and in Catalan "Catalunya".

Through the ages

The road to independence has been long and hard, and the wine industry has had its ups and downs as a result. It's believed that vines were first planted here in the 4th century BC, although it wasn't until the Romans arrived in the 3rd century BC that things really got going.

The industry saw a dip during the occupation by the abstemious Moors, but rose again in the 9th century when the region was united by "Wilfred the Hairy", who established himself as the first independent Count of Barcelona. (As for the name, no one's sure, but it was apparently something to do with the soles of his feet.)

A 12th-century union with Aragón, thanks to the marriage of a subsequent Count of Barcelona to Petronilla of Aragón, marked the beginning of Catalonia's Golden Age. The region flourished and monasteries were built with surrounding vineyards planted and worked by their industrious inhabitants.

In the 15th century, however, there was another setback in Catalonia's mission to remain autonomous when, as a result of more royal nuptials, the region was added to the rest of Spain.

ABOVE *The modernist co-op in L'Espluga de Francolí, Conca de Barberà, is one of the most important in the area.*

WINE STYLES

. . . .

For many centuries Catalonia was known for its hefty, oxidized *rancio* wines and its sweet *vinos de licor*. All that changed beyond recognition in the 1960s when Torres had a big hand in **revolutionizing Spanish wine**. (*See* the full story on p.123). **Almost every style of wine known to man is now produced in Catalonia.** From red, white, and rosé, still and sparkling, dry and intensely sweet, you'll find whatever your heart desires here.

The 20th century

A brief glimmer of hope was offered by a new Republican government in 1931, but was soon snatched away by General Franco who, after the Civil War, even banned the Catalan language in an attempt to tame these unruly people. The spirit of the Catalans was too strong to be forever quashed, though, and they finally won through in the late 1970s to the self-government they enjoy today.

Independence has therefore been hard won in this land of rocky coastlines, golden beaches, undulating vineyards, and towering mountains, which can finally express its unique and fascinating personality to the full. Maybe it's because of this, along with the magnificent Barcelona Olympics of 1992, that Catalonia is currently one of the most popular destinations in Spain.

Catalonia today

In the new Spanish Constitution of 1978, Catalonia became an autonomous community incorporating the four provinces of Barcelona, Gerona, Lérida, and Tarragona. Within these four provinces there lie 11 separate wine DOs, one DOCa, and a couple of areas producing *vino de la tierra* wines.

In the following chapters we'll travel around seven of the 11 DOs, including the superior DOCa (DOQ) region of Priorat. Our destinations will be Costers del Segre, Conca de Barberà, Priorat, Montsant, Tarragona, Penedès, and Empordà-Costa Brava.

DO Catalunya

You're likely, on your travels, to come across wines that are labelled simply "DO Catalunya". The denomination was granted in 1999 and there's a website (www.do-catalunya.com) where you can find out everything from when winemaking began in Catalonia to information on public tours of the DO's Control Board.

DO Catalunya wines can be made from a mixture of grapes grown anywhere within the established DO wine regions, as well as grapes grown according to the rules of DO Catalunya but outside the individual DOs. In practice, and for various different reasons, most of Catalonia's well-known wineries produce wines under this generic label. Cava houses use it for their still wines, others for regional blends, and just one or two pioneering individuals take advantage of the flexibility it offers when they find the strict regulations of their local DO too stifling.

Costers del Segre

A s you pass from Aragón into the western extremities of Catalonia, you'll find yourself in one of its least-known wine regions, the Costers del Segre. The land here is flat and arid, with summer temperatures reaching heights that can leave you pretty hot under the collar and gagging for a refreshing glass or two of the local *vino*.

The region
Costers del Segre is in the province of Lérida, which centres on a town of the same name. Here you'll find an old cathedral perched on a hill that offers spectacular views of the surrounding countryside. The modern wine industry in the region is young, but quality is generally high and the local food you'll be served to accompany it will be hearty enough to guarantee there'll be no one reaching for the biscuit tin.

Raimat story
Around a century ago, a man with a dream bought a piece of barren land and a derelict castle. His somewhat ambitious goal was to make wine of the very highest quality. But this was no ordinary man, and almost 100 years later his investment is far from the unpromising piece of scrubland of those early days.

The man in question was Manuel Raventós and his story is inextricably linked with the rise of the Costers del Segre to its position of respect, if not exactly worldwide fame, within the wine-producing regions of Spain today. The Raventós family were already hugely successful producers of cava in Penedès, to the east of Catalonia (*see* p.126 under Codorníu – Raimat is part of Grupo Codorníu), and Raventós saw the potential to create another successful estate where others had previously feared to tread. Although the area had been planted to vines in the past, the quality just wasn't good enough to warrant replanting after phylloxera hit Spain towards the end of the 19th century.

The Costers del Segre has a continental climate and no more than 400mm (15.7 inches) of annual rainfall – additional water is therefore vital for the successful nurturing of healthy vines here. When Raventós bought the Lérida estate in 1914, he knew that the construction of the Aragón and Catalonia canal would finally allow the land to be irrigated and render his Raimat estate fertile enough for vines. The name, incidentally, was derived from a picture of grapes (*raim*) and a hand (*ma*) inscribed on a 17th-century stone slab which was found at the property. Water wasn't, however, the only requirement; the

USEFUL INFORMATION

Turisme de Lleida (Lérida)
Major 31 Bis
25007 Lleida
Tel: +34 902 250 050
www.paeria.es/turisme
A very good website
about the city.

www.xtec.es/~dcastel/
catalu/costsegr.html
This site isn't great, but
it's the closest the DO gets
to offering information
on the wineries.

composition of the soil was such that years of restructuring would be needed before vines could flourish.

Over the next couple of decades, poplar trees and other crops were planted in order to change the structure of the soil, and irrigation channels were dug to provide water for the land. In order to accommodate the large team of workers that such a project demanded, houses were erected and roads were built. In 1918, the final piece was placed in the jigsaw of Raventós' vision, as Rubió i Bellver of the Gaudí school of architecture was commissioned to construct a magnificent winery, reputedly the first reinforced concrete building in Spain.

The long-awaited first harvest of 1930 yielded only five baskets of fruit. Undeterred by this rather unimpressive start, business continued as usual, and over the years Raimat has grown and prospered beyond anything that could have been initially imagined – Raimat's turnover in 2004 topped 20 million euros. In 1988 Domingo Triay was commissioned to design a new state-of-the-art "underground" winery, which he did by levelling a small hill, building a new winery in its place, encasing it in the removed earth, and topping it off with a vineyard. In this way the temperature is controlled under an attractive blanket of vines. Today Raimat continues to dominate the region and still owns over half of the vines. It also remains at the forefront of technical innovation both in the vineyards and in the winemaking process, and it's fair to say that the DO Costers del Segre wouldn't as yet exist were it not for the work of Raimat.

Route: East from Lérida
90km (56 miles)

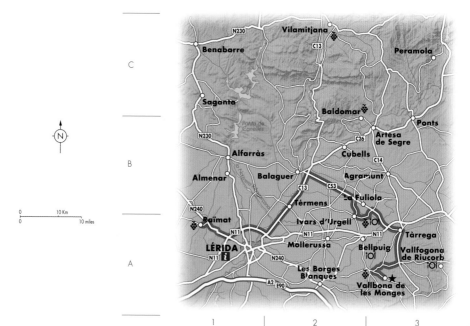

0   10 Km
0   10 miles

DO and the sub-zones

After the usual delays and official wrangling, the DO for this sprawling region was finally granted in 1988. Its six sub-zones, which circle the town of Lérida, cover a total of just 4,180ha and there are around 20 member bodegas, including a handful of cooperatives. Heading in a clockwise direction the sub-zones are: Pallars Jussà; Artesa de Segre; Valls du Riucorb; Les Garrigues; Raimat; and Segrià. The smallest is Raimat, although it has the most land under vine, and I'd suggest you drop in on this sub-zone and at least two or three others to get a feel for the place.

A large mixture of international and indigenous varieties is grown throughout the region, with Chardonnay and the cava trio (see p.19) dominating white wine production, whilst Cabernet Sauvignon, Merlot, Pinot Noir, Garnacha, and Tempranillo (often referred to here as "Gotim Bru" or "Brown Bunch") tend to be most in favour for the reds. Production is small-scale and quality-driven.

ABOVE *Raimat's new space-age winery stands next to, and in complete contrast with, the old modernist facility.*

Getting there

Lérida is around 150km (93 miles) west of Barcelona and there's a regular train service (www.renfe.es) which can take anything from two to four hours, so remember to check the timetable if you'd rather not end up on "snail rail". Buses also run regularly from Barcelona (tel: +34 932 656 506) and take a similar amount of time as the faster trains.

Again, the most efficient way to travel around is to have

WHERE TO EAT
. . . .
El Pages del Coscollar [A2/3]
SCP, Afores, Bellpuig
25250 Lleida
Tel: +34 973 251 082
Robust meat-based dishes are the order of the day.

ABOVE *A modernist archway at Raimat (see previous page).*

RIGHT *Inside the Sanctuary at Castell del Remei.*

your own four wheels. So if you can, pick up a hire car at the airport and then take either the main A2/E90 motorway which goes via the Conca de Barberà region, or, if you want to avoid tolls, the slightly smaller N11 which runs to the north of and parallel to the A2.

Travelling around

Route summary The route begins with a visit to Raimat, to the west of Lérida. It then heads east above the town and out to La Fuliola in the Artesa de Segre sub-zone, before dropping down into Valls du Riucorb for another visit and a night of pampering. The route is approximately 90km (56 miles). Note: An alternative would be to go north, rather than south, from La Fuliola, where you'll find two of the suggested bodegas and a different choice of hotel.

Route: east from Lérida

The first thing you'll see on a visit to Raimat is the old Gaudí-inspired *modernista* winery sitting in the shadow of the new "glass box" facility – the latter was built towards the end of the last century and it's fascinating to see how styles of architecture can change so radically in the space of 80 years. Raimat is also the place to learn about technical innovation in winemaking, as the estate is responsible for research and development within the whole of the Codorníu group and acts as a leading light for other producers throughout the region. As we've talked a lot about Raimat already, let's move swiftly on to another excellent bodega, Castell del Remei.

A hearty lunch

From Raimat drop down on the N240 and pick up the N11 going east above Lérida. Having circled the top of the town, head northeast on the C13 towards Balaguer. Turn right onto the C53 and, just before you reach La Fuliola, take another right to Ivars d'Urgell and there's a sign directing you to the winery. Castell del Remei has been owned by the Cusine family since 1982. The winery was constructed in the 19th century and was in its heyday some time before the Raimat project was even begun. From the middle of the 20th century, however, things fell into disrepair and it was only with the change of ownership that new life was breathed into the estate. The castle is empty, as all efforts so far have been focused on regenerating the vineyards, but possible

WHERE TO STAY

Hotel Can Boix [C3]
C/Afores s/n
25790 Peramola
(L'Alt Urgell)
Tel: +34 973 470 266
www.canboix.com
hotel@canboix.com

Hotel Regina Spa [A3]
Ctra Del Balneari 13km
43427 Vallfogona
de Riucorb
Conca de Barberà
Tel: +34 977 880 028
info@hotel-
balneariregina.com
www.hotel-
balneariregina.com

future plans include its transformation into a smart hotel. There's a sanctuary if you fancy tying the knot amongst vines, and a very good restaurant serving substantial portions of home-cooked local food – just the ticket after a hard morning's tasting. Lérida's cuisine often includes pork in the form of sausages and stews, along with snails, grilled meats, local olive oil, and lots of fresh fruit.

Of the wines produced here, the Castell del Remei Gotim Bru (a blend of Tempranillo, Merlot, and Cabernet Sauvignon) is perhaps the most complete, not too heavy and with intriguing sour cherry fruit. Remei also makes a stunning range of wines, further south and towards the border with Priorat, known as Cérvoles (the Catalan word for deer). There are three wines, a white and two reds, ranging from 18–45 euros. They're not cheap, but then great wines rarely are.

Social awareness

From La Fuliola drop down south on the C53 and onto the C14 via Tàrrega. Take a right onto the small L201 and then turn left down to Vallbona de les Monges. Here you'll find the L'Olivera cooperative, an extraordinary project which was begun in the 1970s to help disadvantaged local people, especially the poor and mentally handicapped, to learn about farming and agriculture. Winemaking here is small-scale, focused on whites and, as you would imagine, conducted in a socially and environmentally friendly way.

Having just witnessed the honourable and self-sacrificing work of others, perhaps a few moments of quiet contemplation are called for, and what better place could there be for such reflection than the local convent of Vallbona de les Monges? (Tel: +34 977638 329; www.larutadelcister.info) The building, which dates from the 12th century, is home to a community of Cistercian nuns and is unique in that it's been occupied, other than in times of war, for over 800 years.

Time to be pampered

The Hotel Regina Spa sits on the border between the Costers del Segre and Conca de Barberà regions, and is therefore ideally placed for touring either of the areas. Hidden deep in the forest just beyond the village of Vallfogona de Riucorb, it sits quietly by the twisting roadside waiting to welcome guests in search of ultimate peace and relaxation. Here you can gaze out at the dramatic surrounding countryside as you drift quietly in the outdoor pool, or alternatively opt for the indoor spa, where alongside a large jacuzzi you'll find treatment rooms offering massages and other such indulgences. The food is superb and each evening you can choose between a 40-euro *dégustación* menu, the *a la carte*, and a *tapas*-style self service table packed with local cheeses, salamis, olives, and sardines.

BODEGAS IN
COSTERS DEL SEGRE

Castell del Remei [A2/3]
25333 Lleida
Tel: +34 973 580 200
carlos@castelldelremei.com

Cooperativa L'Olivera [A3]
Vallbona de les
Monges s/n
25198 Lleida
Tel: +34 973 330 276
www.olivera.org
olivera@olivera.org

Raimat [A1]
Afueras s/n
25111 Raimat (Lleida)
Tel: +34 973 724000
www.raimat.com
info@raimat.com

Vall de Baldomar [B2/C3]
La Font
25737 Baldomar
Tel: +34 932 851 783
valdomar@smc.es

Vila Corona [C2]
Camí els Nerets s/n
25654 Vilamitjana
Lleida
Tel: +34 973 652 638
vila-corona@teleline.es

Conca de Barberà

The "Conca" of the name describes the topography of this little area, which is a bowl-shaped river valley, protected on all sides by valley walls and the various mountain ranges above them. However pocket-sized the region may be, it's packed with things to see and do, and whether it's monasteries, wine, walking, or caves that most interest you, you'll find them all within its pretty confines.

Dug from a foundation of fizz

In the past, the region's combination of chalky limestone soils and semi-Mediterranean climate was deemed perfect for the production of grapes and base wines for cava, which it supplied to its rather more famous neighbour, Penedès. Since the formation of the DO in 1989, however, and the subsequent classification of Catalunya as a DO, there's been major investment in the region, and today you'll find some very classy wines being produced from Conca de Barberà grapes.

Getting there

This is one region where, as long as you pack your walking boots or hire a bicycle, there are plenty of options whether you have your own car or not. Regional trains run from Barcelona to Montblanc – the region's main town – or L'Espluga de Francolí, from where the Monestir de Poblet is a 3km (2-mile) walk. Alternatively you could take a fast train (www.renfe.es; 45 mins–1 hour 15 mins) to Tarragona and then travel by bus (Vivasa Buses, tel: +34 902 101 363) to Montblanc or L'Espluga de Francolí – this way you can even stop off at the Monestir on the way.

BELOW *Around the Monestir de Poblet you'll find beautiful scenery and peaceful roads, ideal for cyclists.*

It's around 115km (71.5 miles) from Barcelona to Montblanc and, in spite of what I've already said, travelling by car will of course allow you the freedom to see more of the local wineries and vineyards.

Travelling around

Route One summary Beginning at the Monestir de Poblet, this route moves on to L'Espluga de Francolí, then continues east, via Montblanc, to Barberà de la Conca. From here you carry on up to Sarral and Rocafort de Queralt, before dropping back down to

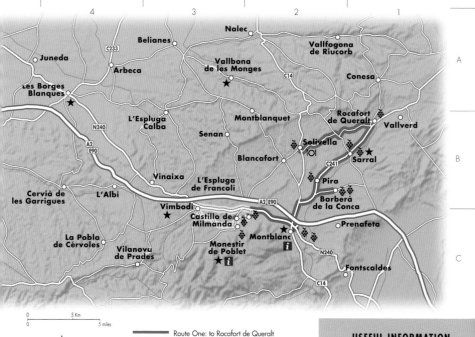

Route One: to Rocafort de Queralt
50km (31 miles)

Route Two: the pedestrian route
13.5km (8.4 miles)

0   5 Km
0   5 miles

N

finish in Solivella. You can then choose to head either north or south for the evening. This route is around 50km (31 miles).

Route Two summary This short walking route covers a triangle which begins at the Monestir de Poblet and Castillo de Milmanda, heads east to L'Espluga de Francolí, and then west to Vimbodí, before returning to the Monestir. This route is 13.5km (8.4 miles) and is well signposted.

Route One: to Rocafort de Queralt
The imposing Monasterio de Santa Maria de Poblet dates from the 12th century and, along with Vallbona de les Monges and Santes Creus, forms part of the local route of Cistercian monasteries (www.larutadelcister.info).

Although a monastic community was founded here in 1153, the monastery was abandoned for a century following the expulsion of the monks in 1835. Fortunately, the Patrinage of Poblet saw fit to sponsor its renovation at the beginning of the 20th century and today you'll find a small community of monks, the Brotherhood of Poblet, living and working within its walls. You can take a guided tour of the monastery and even drop in on a service, but we're here for the wine and it's to be found at the Abadía de Poblet winery.

The Cistercians had been making wine here since the Middle Ages, but it was only with their departure from Poblet

USEFUL INFORMATION

Consejo Regulador de Conca de Barberà
C/Sant Josep 18
43400 Montblanc
Tel: +34 977 861 232
www.do-conca.org

Municipal Tourism Office
Antiga Esgl de St Francesco
43400 Montblanc
Tel: +34 977 861 733

Municipal Tourism Office
C Torres Jordi 16
43440 L'Espluga de Francolí
Tel: +34 977 871 220
Call for tours of **Palaeolithic** and **Neolithic caves.**

Regional Tourism Office
Passeig de l'Abat Conill 9B
43448 Poblet
Tel: +34 977 871 247

Walking tours
Alberg de Joventut Jaume 1
Ctra de Les Masies s/n
43440 L'Espluga de Francolí
Tel: +34 977 871 732

www.conca.altanet.org for information on the region.

in 1835 that the winery was established. It was just after this time, around the middle of the 19th century, that a family called Girona came into possession of some land adjacent to the monastery. This family was responsible for developing farming and for constructing a building in 1870 to process the oil, cereal crops, fruit, and wine produced by the property. Over 100 years later, in 1980, the Raventós family (see p.93) sought and gained the monks' permission to plant vineyards within the monastery walls. They chose Pinot Noir and planted 9ha, whilst at the same time employing the company's preferred architect, Domingo Triay, to restore the old winery.

The 19th-century farm building is today both a winery and a shop (tel: +34 977 870 358; 11am–2pm and 4–6.30pm daily). It sells just the one wine, which is only for sale here and in local restaurants. The first vintage of Abadía de Poblet Pinot Noir was 2002 and 15,000 –20,000 bottles are produced annually.

A taste of Torres

Torres is a Catalan company based in the neighbouring region of Penedès, and although it doesn't as yet have a winery in Conca de Barberà, it's here that the grapes for some of the company's best wines are grown.

Tucked behind the Monestir de Poblet is the Muralles estate, which surrounds a very special 32ha single vineyard. From this small parcel of indigenous vines come the hand-picked grapes for one of Torres' top red wines, Grans Muralles, and a wander through this stunning vineyard may be the deciding factor as you later consider investing in a bottle.

Torres owns 350ha of vines in Conca de Barberà, split between the four estates of Gran Muralles, Riudabella, Mas de Baix, and Milmanda. One of owner Miguel Torres' passions is the propagation of ancient Catalan grape varieties, and in 1985 he planted several here as part of an ongoing campaign (which includes placing adverts in local newspapers) to seek them out.

BODEGAS IN CONCA DE BARBERA

Agrícola i Secció de Crèdit Espluga [C2/3]
(Architect: Pere Domènech i Roura, 1913)
C/Josep M Rendé 5
43440 L'Espluga de Francolí
Tel: +34 977 870 105
coespluga@retemail.es

Antoni Sans Español (Caves Santravé) [B2]
C/de la Conca 10
43412 Solivella
Tel: +34 977 892 165
www.sanstrave.com

Cooperativa Agrícola de Barberà de la Conca [B1/2]
(Architect: Cèsar Martinell, 1917)
Pl Hospital 24
43422 Barberà de la Conca
Tel: +34 977 887 035

Cooperativa Agrícola de Rocafort de Queralt [B1]
(Architect: Cèsar Martinell, 1918)
Av Catalunya 35
43426 Rocafort de Queralt
Tel: +34 977 898 005
corocafort@do-conca.org

continued opposite

A royal favourite

Just a short distance from Poblet is another Torres property, the medieval Castle of Milmanda. Here, for 3 euros, you'll be shown an introductory video, given a tour of the 13th-century tower with its sweeping panorama of vineyards, and offered a complimentary glass of Chardonnay. Quaffable as it may be, it's a far cry from the estate's single-vineyard, barrel-fermented Milmanda, which costs 30 euros a bottle and was the wine chosen for the wedding of Prince Philippe in May 2004. The wines are not, however, all prohibitively expensive and the range sold in the castle's shop includes many cheaper bottles with which to fill your boot.

Modernista madness

Following the devastating effect of the phylloxera bug on the region's vineyards towards the end of the 19th century, local farmers had to think of some way to pool resources in order to survive such difficult times. The solution they came up with was remarkable on two fronts, firstly because it led to the pioneering of the cooperative movement in winemaking throughout the region, and secondly because the buildings created to house these cooperative wineries were shortly to become important works of art.

"Modernism", a movement which finds its greatest expression in the architectural works of Antoni Gaudí, was fast inspiring Catalonia's young artists, and the cooperative wineries were designed according to this innovative style. Although they may lack the fairytale "gingerbread house" colour and curves of some of Gaudí's most compelling works, they make use of the sweeping parabolic arches and stained glass mosaics, as well as the lofty interiors synonymous with this expressive period.

It was, in fact, just such features that led to these buildings being dubbed the "Cathedrals of Wine". Undoubtedly, one of the most impressive can be found in L'Espluga de Francolí, where the shopkeeper will fill your plastic

BODEGAS IN CONCA DE BARBERA (CONTINUED)

Codorníu (Abadía de Poblet) [C2/3]
Passeig de l'Abat Conill 6
43448 Poblet (Vimbodí)
Tel: +34 977 870 358
www.codorniu.es

Concavins [B1/2]
Ctra Montblanc –
Barberà s/n
43422 Barberà
de la Conca
Tel: +34 977 887 030
www.bodegasconcavins.com

Cooperativa de Viticultors i Ca de Montblanc [C2] (Architect: Cèsar Martinell, 1919)
Muralla Sta Tecla 54–56
43400 Montblanc
Tel: +34 977 860 016
www.cavapontvell.com

Cooperativa Vinícola de Sarral [B1/2] (Architect: Pere Domènech i Roura, 1914)
Av de la Conca 33
43424 Sarral
Tel: +34 977 890 031
cavaportell@covisal.es

Mas Foraster [C2]
Camí de St Josep s/n
43400 Montblanc
Tel: +34 977 860 229

Miguel Torres [C2/3]
Castillo de Milmanda
Ctra de L'Espluga de
Francolí – Poblet 2.5km
43430 Vimbodí
Tel: +34 619 831 314
www.torreswines.com

Rosa Maria Torres [B1/2]
Av D'Anguera, 2
43424 Sarral
Tel: +34 977 890 013

ABOVE LEFT The Cistercian Monestir de Poblet.

LEFT The cooperative in Solivella.

WHERE TO STAY

**Alojamientos Rurales El Clos
[A1]** C/Rocafort 12
43427 Conesa
Tel: +34 977 898 021

Fonda Cal Blasi [C2]
C/Alenyà 11
43400 Montblanc
Tel: +34 977 861 336
www.fondacalblasi.com

Hostal Fonoll [C2/3]
Ramon Berenguer IV 2
43448 Poblet
Tel: +34 977 870 333

Hostal de Senglar [C2/3]
Plaça Montserrat Canals 1
43440 L'Espluga
de Francolí
Tel: +34 977 870 121
www.hostaldelsenglar.com

Hotel Regina Spa [A3]
See the box on p.96.

Monestir de Poblet [C2/3]
Tel: +34 977 870 254
for tours and information
www.poblet_pviana.com
A new hostelry is being built
within the monastery walls.

water bottle with local wine for less than a euro a litre, and then offer you a tour of the small on-site museum.

I'd suggest that you visit all the cooperative wineries at the weekend, when you're more likely to find someone who will be willing to show you around. As we progress along the route I'll point out the villages with cooperative cellars and you can either drop in at one or two as part of your general wine tour, or devote a separate day to visiting all of them. I've listed the most important ones (see the boxes on p.100 and p.101) along with the architect who designed them and the date of construction.

You may decide to stay in the fortified medieval town of Montblanc, which, along with its Gothic and Romanesque monuments, is home to the Mas Foraster winery. For a century and a half the Foraster family has grown vines and olives in the region and in 1998 a small winery was finally built. Today the family produces a limited quantity of top-quality red wines from the surrounding Cabernet Sauvignon and Tempranillo vines.

All in the name

From here the route heads north up the T242 to the town which gave the region its name, Barberà de la Conca. There's a cooperative winery here as well as Bodegas Concavins, which used to be a co-op itself until it was privatized in 1988. This is now a sophisticated, bang-up-to date operation which provides perfect contrast to the delightful rurality of the local "bring your own bottle" bodegas. Concavins produces a wide range of still wines from indigenous and international varieties, as well as Catalonia's traditional sparkling cava.

Alabaster

From here you head west to pick up the C241 north via Pira, Sarral, and Rocafort de Queralt, all of which have their own *modernista* co-op. In Sarral you'll also find Rosa Maria Torres (try the Susel Cabernet Franc/Syrah) and the Museu de l'Alabastre (tel: +34 977 890 158), for stocking up on non wine-related gifts. I have to confess that I didn't actually know what alabaster was, although I had heard the word used in reference to fairytale princesses with impossibly clear skin. It's apparently a translucent, usually white, form of gypsum (the mineral used to make plaster of Paris), which is carved into ornaments that you may or may not manage to squeeze into your wine-loaded luggage.

For your final stop, head back to the C14 and Solivella. Here you'll find Caves Santravé, a small bodega with its own restaurant called Cal Travé.

Route Two: the pedestrian route

This is a short walk, ideal for a lovely sunny day. Begin with the Monestir de Poblet and Castillo de Milmanda, as above, and then walk across to L'Espluga de Francolí, where you can visit the cooperative and have a bite to eat. From here cross west to Vimbodí, which has a glass museum and school – if anyone fancies brushing up on their glass-blowing technique. And finally you can stroll back down to your starting point at Poblet.

Well oiled

If you're an olive oil fan then there's a small route of local farms which you can follow. Start out at Les Borges Blanques (where there's a museum; map ref: A4), move on to Arbeca, then L'Espluga Calba, and finally Vinaixa.

A Spanish welcome

I learned, whilst in this region, that if you see a cypress tree in front of a house you'll be welcome to spend the night, if it's an olive tree there'll be a meal on offer, and if there's no tree at all, it's time to move on.

Wild boar

Known as "sanglar" in Catalan, wild boar is a speciality of this region's cuisine. It is slow-cooked in local red wine until meltingly tender, and is then served with potatoes, tomatoes, and peppers. I also have it on good authority that it's traditional to add a splash of the boar's blood towards the end of cooking.

ABOVE AND LEFT *Close to the monastery at Poblet, the Castillo de Milmanda with its 13th-century tower was acquired by Torres in the 1970s.*

WHERE TO EAT

This isn't an area with lots of great restaurants, so eating in your hotel may be the best option.

Fonda Cal Blasi [C2]
See the box opposite.

Hostal Fonoll [C2/3]
See the box opposite.

Hostal de Senglar [C2/3]
Great for the wild boar mentioned on the left.
See the box opposite.

Hotel Regina Spa [A3]
See the box on p.96.

Restaurant Cal Travé [B2]
C/Artesa 56
43412 Solivella
restaurant@sanstrave.com

Priorat

Priorat, the indisputable jewel in Spain's winemaking crown, is magical, mystical, and utterly exquisite. The history that lies behind some of Spain's most sensual wines is as intriguing as the liquid itself, and the journey you'll be taking through the vines and wines of this unique region will intoxicate and delight from the moment you set foot on its precious slate soil.

Moving around Montsant

Priorat is a small, sleepy region, hidden in the hills to the southwest of Barcelona in the province of Tarragona. The younger DO of Montsant virtually surrounds it and many of the recommended bodegas, restaurants, and hotels are applicable for either place, so I'd suggest you spend three or four days here and drive all three routes (two of which are detailed here, and one is in the following chapter, p.115). That way you'll not only get a proper feel for the place and its stunning scenery, you'll also taste enough wines to appreciate the difference between the rich, heady style of Priorat and the lighter, more precocious one of Montsant.

BELOW An iron sculpture in the centre of Gratallops.

Past, present, and future

For many years Priorat was one of Catalonia's poorest regions, dependent on agriculture for its living and yet an area of dry, rocky, unyielding land. As a result, when foreign tourists discovered the delights of the Spanish *costas* during the 1960s and 1970s, Priorat's disillusioned youngsters made a dash for the coast in order to cash in on this new source of income. The wine industry they left behind was already in a poor state of repair, with old methods of production yielding tired, unclean wines in scruffy old cooperative cellars. With the departure of this generation, things only looked set to worsen.

But instead something, or perhaps I should say someone, rather special happened to Priorat. In 1989, 25-year-old Alvaro Palacios arrived from Rioja, where he'd been working in his family business Palacios Remondo with René Barbier. Barbier himself had returned to Gratallops ten years earlier and together they joined forces with Carles Pastrana (Costers del Siurana), José Luis Pérez (Mas Martinet, and also one of Catalonia's most revered oenologists and viticulturists), and Dafne Glorian (Clos Erasmus), in what was a sort of 'hippy' cooperative venture. The group determined to make one wine, from their best grapes, which they each would market separately under their own label.

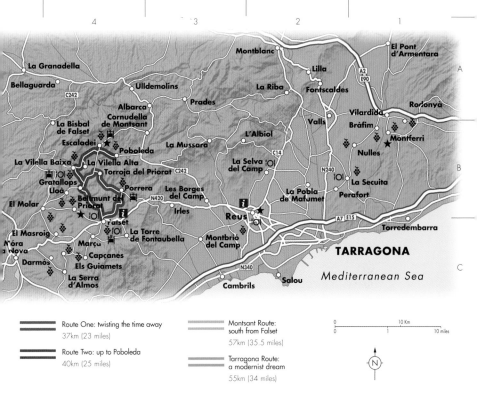

Route One: twisting the time away
37km (23 miles)

Route Two: up to Poboleda
40km (25 miles)

Montsant Route:
south from Falset
57km (35.5 miles)

Tarragona Route:
a modernist dream
55km (34 miles)

0   10 Km
0   10 miles

N

The first vintage was 1989 and the response from the wine world was staggering. What these pioneers had was superb material to work with – in the form of old-vine Garnacha and Cariñena – that had been crying out for some decent winemakers to get their hands on. Today each estate is famous in its own right with Palacios' L'Ermita wine (from the famous vineyard of the same name) commanding the highest prices in a seriously expensive line-up.

Tiger-skin slate

Priorat's best wines are a luxurious and seductive mix of rich, velvety, dark fruits and tenacious minerality, with a streak of fresh acidity underpinning each heady mouthful. The alcohol levels are high and the tannins soft, yet rarely do you feel either is out of balance and the temptation to drain the bottle is always strong. Although the old vines are important, the soil in which they're grown also plays its part in the formation of these delicious wines. Llicorella is the name of the stripey red/grey slate, rich in iron oxide, that flanks each twisting road. Unlike other forms of slate which are acidic in composition, llicorella is virtually neutral, and it's this neutrality which allows the grape vines planted in it to absorb minerals more easily.

Alongside the old Garnacha and Cariñena growing here, you'll find new plantings of Cabernet Sauvignon, Merlot, and Syrah, which are considered good blending partners for the existing old vines.

Wine facts

In 2003 Priorat was only the second demarcated area in Spain (after Rioja) to be elevated from DO to DOQ (DOCa) status (see p.25). Its total area of cultivation covers around 3,400 hectares. The 2002 harvest was poor, whereas 2004 was excellent.

Tourism in Priorat

The march towards accommodating wine tourists is almost as fast today as the speed at which the new wines rocketed to stardom some 15 years ago. With a realization that their best asset, wine, is almost as appealing to tourists as golden beaches and clear blue seas, the locals are fast waking up to the prospective financial rewards that tourism can offer. Old houses are being converted into small rural hotels, walking routes are being cleared, audio guides are being prepared, and wine cellars are beginning, at last, to open their doors. There's still some way to go and the doors to some of the best cellars as yet remain firmly shut, but the signs are good and you'll definitely find plenty to see and do.

ABOVE *Look out for this tiger-skin, Llicorella slate which is in part responsible for the unique character of Priorat's wines.*

RIGHT *Despite its rise to fame since Priorat's new wave of cult wines, Gratallops remains one of the most unassuming and sleepy villages imaginable.*

Getting there

From Barcelona it takes one and a half hours to drive the 73km (45-mile) journey to Falset via the main C32 motorway and the N420 – the latter is the national road, which you pick up just outside Reus. If you want to avoid tolls, then the national road does run all the way from Barcelona, parallel to the main motorway and a little closer to the coast. You can also fly very cheaply with Ryanair to Reus airport (www.ryanair.com), where it's possible to hire a car (www.carhireexpress.co.uk).

Travelling around

Allow more time than usual for journeys in this area, as the roads tend to be very small and winding.

Route One summary Beginning in Falset, this route twists up to Porrera and then across through Torroja del Priorat to Gratallops, and then back down to Falset. The route is approximately 37km (23 miles).

Route Two summary Again this route begins in Falset and heads straight up through Gratallops to La Vilella Baixa. It then travels northeast to La Vilella Alta, Escaladei, and across to Poboleda. It's around 40km (25 miles).

Route One: twisting the time away

As you climb over the last ridge and sweep down into Falset, it doesn't appear to be especially large or lively by anyone's standards. However, that's until you compare it to Gratallops, Porrera, or any of the little villages that cling to the rugged hillsides of the surrounding area, and are quiet almost to the point of being spooky.

Falset has a fantastically helpful tourist office where you'll be given information on just about anything you might want to know, plus a local map detailing bodegas, restaurants, hotels, and more. The town has an excellent wine shop (Aguiló Vinateria), which also sells a wide selection of regional oils, vinegars, and nuts, along with a handful of good restaurants, a stunning *modernista cooperativo*, and a very useful petrol station.

The only problem is that there's really only one hotel, Hostal Sport, which is acceptable but hasn't any of the charm or attention to detail you'll find, for example, in Hostal Antic Priorat (*see* Route Two, p.111), just outside Poboleda. Equally if you decide to stay in one of the smaller villages such as Gratallops, the quality of accommodation is very basic, and finding a decent dinner on any night but Saturday is virtually impossible – cafés and restaurants open for breakfast (a very social affair) and lunch, but not usually dinner. So in order to benefit from Falset's amenities, as well as to see the local winery workers breakfasting on huge *jamón* baguettes and copious quantities of red wine (at the café just beyond Hostal Sport), I'd suggest you stay a couple of nights here and then a couple of nights somewhere a little more rural.

Route One heads out of Falset towards Gratallops and almost immediately takes a right turn up to Porrera. This road

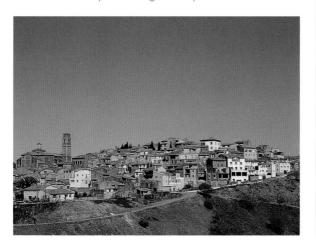

BODEGAS IN PRIORAT OPEN FOR VISITS

Buil i Giné [B4]
Ctra Gratallops
Vilella Baixa 11.5km
43717 Gratallops
Tel: +34 977 830 483
www.builgine.com

Celler Cecilio [B4]
Piró 28
43737 Gratallops
Tel: +34 977 839 507
cellercecilio@hotmail.com

**Celler Joan Sangenis/
Cal Pla [B4]**
Prat de la Riba 1
43739 Porrera
Tel: +34 977 828 125
joan.sangenis@terra.es

Cellers Scala Dei [B4]
Rambla de la Cartoixa s/n
43379 Escaladei
Tel: +34 977 827 027
www.grupocodorniu.com

Cellers de la Cartoixa [B4]
Ereta 10
43375 La Vilella Alta
Tel: +34 977 839 136
correu@cellerscartoixa.com

Costers del Siurana [B4]
Camí Manyetes s/n Pol 11
43737 Gratallops
Tel: +34 977 839 276
www.costersdelsiurana.com

Genium Celler [B4]
Nou 92 Baixos
43376 Poboleda
Tel: +34 977 827 146
www.geniumceller.com

Mas Doix [B4]
C/del Carme 115
43376 Poboleda
Tel: +34 977 827 040
masdoix@bsab.com

Sangenís i Vaqué [B4]
Plaça Catalunya 3
43739 Porrera
Tel: +34 977 828 238

Prices for visits and tastings range from free to €20.

is extremely twisty and the 10km (6-mile) journey will probably seem longer. When you arrive in the small central square, you're likely to be greeted by the sight of children with dripping ice-creams playing in the late afternoon sun (the best time to see Porrera) and parents or older folks chatting quietly on the surrounding benches. There are three wineries in the village and two of them accept visits. Sangenís i Vaqué is on the square itself and Celler Joan Sangenis is in front of the Teatret restaurant in an old house next to the bridge and to the right of the river.

The latter produces excellent wines under the Mas d'en Compte label. The barrel fermented white, a blend of Garnacha Blanca, Picapoll, Pansal, and Macabeo is a big creamy wine, deeply golden in colour and full of orange spice flavours. The red is unusual for Priorat in that it's a little less powerful than most with a stylish red fruit character that matches food well.

Just over the bridge is Vall Llach, famous not only for its wines, but also for being bought in the early 1990s by the highly political singer/songwriter Lluís Llach and a childhood friend of his. Salus Alvarez, president of the local *consejo regulador*, oversees the running of the winery and the production of its three red wines, the best of which is made entirely from the estate's own grapes (Cariñena, Merlot, and Cabernet Sauvignon) and is known simply as Vall Llach. Visits

BELOW *Alvaro Palacios' stylish new winery is so different from the old buildings of neighbouring Gratallops that it seems to have landed from outer space.*

are not possible here, but you'll find the wines in most of the local shops and restaurants.

Glorious Gratallops

Gratallops is the hilltop haunt of the Priorat pioneers. You'll find Alvaro Palacios, Clos Mogador, Clos Erasmus, and Costers del Siurana all based in this unassuming little village, with Mas Martinet just a stone's throw away on the road back down to Falset.

Of the above "famous five", Costers del Siurana is currently the most willing to accept visitors and as you drive from Porrera, through Torroja del Priorat and on into Gratallops, stick to the road which skirts around the west of the village and you'll see an information point and a sign to the bodega on your right. The estate owns 10 vineyards around Gratallops and one close to Torroja, and you must say in advance if you'd like to see a vineyard.

When you hear that they receive around 3,000 visitors a year it's understandable that they have to charge for visits, and although 20 euros may seem steep for a tour and tasting of four of the better wines, you'll be given the best the estate has to offer. Costers del Siurana also owns the Cellers de Gratallops restaurant and wine shop in the centre of the village, and lunch here can be booked to coincide with your visit.

Just behind Costers del Siurana is Clos Mogador, so you could poke your head around the door and see if anyone's available to show you around there too.

In the centre of town, a couple of doors up from Cellers de Gratallops, is Celler Cecilio, where the delightful Raquel Vicent i Baltesar and her father August will be happy to take you on a tour of their vineyards and winery, followed by a tasting of a couple of wines, all for free. It would, however, be polite to buy the odd bottle from them in return for their time and hospitality.

As you head out of the village towards Falset, the space-age sandy-coloured building up on the hill to your right is Alvaro Palacio's impressive new winery. A little further on, around 6.5km (4 miles) before you reach Falset, you'll pass by Mas Martinet (a tiny road drops down to the right and the winery is visible only if you look back after a couple of hundred metres). Stop and park on the left opposite the little road to the right, and you'll see the unique form of vine training adopted by Sara Pérez of Mas Martinet, a kind of iron hula hoop around which the vines entwine themselves (*see* the photograph on p.112).

Feeding time in Falset

There are a couple of places in Falset which offer reasonably priced lunch menus and at El Cairat you'll pay 11 euros for

WHERE TO EAT

Cellers de Gratallops [B4]*
C/Piró 32
43737 Gratallops
Tel: +34 977 839 036

El Cairat [B/C4]*
Nou 3, 43730 Falset
Tel: +34 977 830 481

El Celler de l'Aspic [B/C4]
C/Miquel Barceló 31
43730 Falset
Tel: +34 977 831 246
cellerdelaspic@terra.es

Hostal La Font [B4]
See box on p.109.

Mas Trucafort [B4]*
C/Falset – Bellmunt 1.5km
Apartat de Correus 28
43730 Falset
Tel: +34 977 830 160

Piró [B4]*
C/Piró 21
43737 Gratallops
Tel: +34 977 839 004
Very traditional food.

Quinoa [B/C4]
C/Miquel Barceló 29
43730 Falset
Tel: +34 977 830 431
Rustic; slightly overpriced.

* Open for lunch only and
maybe Saturday evening.

good traditional food which may include white beans from Sant Pau with roasted onions and *romesco* sauce, followed by fried cod with *escalivada* (a mix of peppers, courgettes, and aubergines in olive oil), and home-made ice-cream for dessert. This isn't the best value you'll find, as the menu doesn't include drinks, but the cooking is particularly good.

For dinner you could do worse than to eat in the Hostal Sport, if you can cope with piped music and gingham tablecloths, that is. There is an extensive and well-priced wine list, as well as some delicious Catalan food. Goats' cheese salad with a selection of local almonds, hazelnuts, walnuts, pine nuts, and raisins with a balsamic reduction may be followed by lamb cutlets and fresh strawberries steeped in sweet red wine.

The restaurant not to be missed, however, is El Celler de l'Aspic. Here a four-course set menu of traditional Priorat food can be adapted to your own tastes and includes an additional *aperitivo*, a cheese course, and a dessert. The menu states that two unspecified wines are included in the 36 euro price, and although that doesn't mean you can choose the most expensive ones on the list, don't be surprised when both bottles are left on your table for you to finish.

One wine which I have to mention because it's such stunning value is Vessants, made by the Falset winery of Capafons-Ossó and only 8 euros at El Celler de l'Aspic. This is a Montsant wine which shows bright red and blackberry fruits along with a savoury, meaty edge that makes it perfect for drinking with food. When you consider that decent Priorat wines start at 20–30 euros on most restaurant lists, you can immediately appreciate Montsant's appeal.

Route Two: up to Poboleda

As both of these routes begin in Falset, you could always start one of them with a visit to the local *modernista* co-op, Agrícola Falset-Marça, which falls within the Montsant DO (*see* p.115 for details).

Take the road up to Gratallops and about a kilometre (two-thirds of a mile) beyond the town you'll discover the brand new winery of Buil i Giné. Opened in the summer of 2005 following a three-year search for the right plot of land and a 3.5-million-euro investment, this ambitious project offers perhaps the most tourist-friendly welcome of any winery in the region. The views from here are some of the best you'll see of Priorat, with a panorama that encompasses five of the local villages. Visits are tailored to suit all tastes and you can even arrange to get married here if you plan well enough in advance. The aim of the winery is to make affordable Priorat wines, as well as the more swanky stuff, and you'll find the basic Giné Giné, (a blend of Cariñena and Garnacha), on local lists for around 7–8 euros.

Village life

The route continues on up to the villages of La Vilella Baixa and La Vilella Alta ("the low village" and "the high village" respectively). Both are delightful, with the first clinging quietly to a hillside and the second sitting on top of one. In La Vilella Alta is the little winery of Cellers de la Cartoixa, which makes its wine in four small houses within the village. Although the reds are predictably the best, the white is interesting for its use of Trepat Blanc, a grape grown by just two or three of the local producers.

The priory

The name Priorat translates as priory and in the next village of Escaladei you'll find the very one, dating back to 1163, after which the region was named. As you drive into the village you'll see the Cellers Scala Dei in front of you, but before you visit, take the road to your right up to the Cartoixa (priory) which is open for public visits all year round (10am–1.30pm, 4–7.30pm in the summer; 10am–1.30pm, 3–5.30pm in the winter). It's a magnificent old terracotta and sand-coloured ruin whose majestic façade is flanked by an avenue of stately cypress trees. The best time to see it is perhaps in the early summer when the ground is awash with a profusion of bright red poppies. In the village itself you'll find the winery mentioned above and the two shops detailed in the box to the right.

A cosy night's sleep

This route finishes in Poboleda and just outside the village you'll find Hostal Antic Priorat, one of the best hotels in the area. The 14 bedrooms are individually designed and come complete with decent bathroom smellies, chocolates, and mineral water. The hotel is run by a young couple, Miguel and Olga, who make a daily trip to Reus market for

LEFT *As you set off from Escaladei to the Cartoixa, look out for the old wine press to your right.*

BELOW *A drop of 100-year-old Garnacha goes into the blend at René Barbier's Clos Mogador.*

USEFUL INFORMATION (CONTINUED)

Oficina de Turismo del Priorat
C/Sant Marcel 2
43730 Falset
Tel: +34 977 830 119
www.priorat.org
Superbly helpful tourist office, with an information screen outside if you visit when it's closed.

Vinícola del Priorat (Gratallops) [B4]
Carrer Piró s/n
43737 Gratallops
Tel: +34 977 839 167
An association of four local co-ops of Gratallops, El Lloar, Vilella Baixa, and Vilella Alta, where they've just built a new wine shop.

Vinum & Co [B4]
Plaça Catalunya 1
43739 Porrera
Tel: +34 977 828 118
www.vinumandco.com
A little wine shop in the main square of Porrera.

www.xtec.es/~dcastel/catalu/priorat.html
Not a great site, but gives details of the DO wineries.

fresh provisions, and if you've chosen to have dinner here (22 euros) you can request your favourite dish before the shopping is done. The hotel is in a beautiful location with 7ha of vineyards and an outdoor pool.

A chance to taste

It may not be possible to visit some of the smaller wineries in the area, but for 5 euros, restaurant Mas Trucafort (just outside Falset on the road to Bellmunt) will arrange for you to taste the wines of nine local producers who've grouped together under the banner of the "Petits Cellers del Priorat". It's a great idea which was spearheaded by owner/chef Roger Felip, and is an unmissable chance to try some of the wines you'll otherwise only see in shops or restaurants. The food here is also terrific value with a three-course lunch including wine, bread, and water costing just 8.50 euros. The tourist office will be happy to ring and arrange a tasting.

Slowly does it

Service is something of a hit and miss affair in these parts, but as long as you don't expect a waiter or waitress to come anywhere near your table until at least 10 minutes after you've been seated, then you won't be disappointed. The menu rarely has an English translation and you may find a small dictionary useful if you want to know your lamb from your duck and your fava beans from your foie gras.

It's also worth mentioning that it's quite expensive by Spanish standards to dine out here, with the steep prices of the wines tending to be mirrored by those of the food. However, when you consider what you'd pay for these wines elsewhere in the world and then take into account the standard of the local cooking, dinner for two at between 50–60 euros is actually pretty good value. A tip: always check if drinks and tax are included, as this can make a considerable difference to your final bill.

Olive green

Another product for which Priorat and Montsant are famous

is olive oil, and there are olive oil "routes" being planned as I write. The majority of the trees are grown to the north of the region, along with almonds and peaches, in terrain that's too dry to sustain vines.

The best oil is made from a small variety of green olive called Arbequina. It yields an unctuous liquid that combines bold, fruity flavours with pepper and cream. Most of the local oil sells from as little as 4 euros a litre and comes under the wide DOP Siurana. (DOP or *Denominación de Origen Protegida* is a protected designation of origin for olive oils.) In a brave move 10 local producers have recently joined together to make one superior oil (a blend of their best olives), which retails at three-and-a-half times the price of the basic stuff. It's called Oleum Priorat and is sold in smart 500ml glass bottles rather than 5-litres plastic ones.

Olive routes aside, if you fancy ditching the car and exploring this area on foot, smart green signs clearly signpost various walking routes throughout the region.

Wine festival

Falset town hall organizes a wine fair, the Mostra de Vins, which takes place along the main street of the town during the first weekend of May each year. Your ticket (8 euros) will entitle you to a glass in a holder that hangs around your neck, and a tasting of five wines. There are also fairs in Poboleda and Porrera.

ABOVE *La Vilella Baixa village.*

LEFT *Vine-training at Mas Martinet.*

BODEGAS IN PRIORAT CLOSED TO VISITS

Tip: an initial "no" can often become a "yes" if you show a keen interest in the wine.

Alvaro Palacios [B4]
43737 Gratallops
Tel: +34 977 839 195

Celler Vall Llach [B4]
C/del Pont 9, 43739 Porrera
Tel: +34 977 828 244
www.vallllach.com

Clos Mogador [B4]
Camí Manyetes
43737 Gratallops
Tel: +34 977 839 171

Mas Martinet [B/C4]
Ctra Falset –
Gratallops 6km
43730 Falset
Tel: +34 629 238 236
www.masmartinet.com

Montsant

The DO of Montsant, named after its majestic backdrop of the Montsant Escarpment, forms an incomplete circle in the shape of the letter "C" around DOCa Priorat. The area was traditionally dominated by cooperative wineries, a partial throwback to post-phylloxera days when working together as a community to revive a devastated industry was essential. At this time Montsant came under the Falset sub-zone of the larger Tarragona DO and a great deal of the wine it produced was sold in bulk. Only in 2001, when it became a DO in its own right, did people begin to see the value of bottling their own wine and aiming for higher quality.

Buying up the land

With Montsant's elevated status has come some canny investment from owners of established Priorat bodegas seeking to maximize the potential of far cheaper land, yet land which still offers enormous diversity and suitability for quality wine production. As you'll notice, Priorat's prized llicorella slate isn't quite so abundant in this outer circle and Montsant's wines don't usually display the power and breeding of their neighbour's, but they're also not weighed down by such hefty price tags.

BELOW *Gnarled old vines give very low yields of wonderfully concentrated fruit.*

On most local wine lists you'll find a wide selection of both Priorat and Montsant wines, so you'll have plenty of opportunity to compare styles and prices before deciding for yourself if you consider Priorat's "premium" is a price worth paying. What you may find is that the wines of Priorat, with their voluptuous texture and rich, dark, creamy flavours, are wonderful to sip on their own, whereas food is better suited to the rusticity and racy, red fruit character of Montsant.

As you travel the route detailed below you'll visit a variety of cooperatives and a selection of smaller, family-owned estates. It's interesting not only to compare these two types of operation, but also to see how the co-ops are changing and improving as the name of Montsant becomes better known and the potential to cash in on the quality wine market becomes a reality. Montsant has around 1,900ha under vine.

Getting there *See* p.106.

Travelling around
Route summary This route begins in Falset, like the Priorat routes. But instead of heading north, it drops down south through Marçà to Capçanes and on to Els Guiamets. It then continues south through La Serra d'Almos and up to Darmós, El Masroig, and El Molar. It returns to Falset via Bellmunt del Priorat, which falls within the Priorat DOQ. The route is 57km (35.5 miles).

ABOVE *The quiet streets of Falset are home to some of the region's best restaurants – and they open on week nights, which is virtually unheard of elsewhere.*

Route: south from Falset
The Agrícola Falset-Marçà winery was designed by modernista architect Cèsar Martinell and is situated just off the main N420 road west out of Falset – if you can't find it just ask in the *cooperativo's* shop next to Celler de l'Aspic on Miquel Barceló. One of the specialities here is a traditional local wine known as "rancí". It's definitely an acquired taste and as Robert Veyga Alonso of the co-op says, "You have to be Catalan to love this stuff." It's a 15–16% alcohol wine which is oxidized in demi-johns outside on the roof for a year (make sure you ask to see these) and then matured in old barrels for at least two years, and sometimes up to 40. All the wines, vinegars, vermouths, and oils which the co-op produces can be bought in the shop.

Whilst in Falset, you could also drop in on Capafons-Ossó, a winery that makes wines under both Priorat and Montsant denominations – the estate is difficult to find so ask for directions.

Head south from Falset, past Marçà, and on to Capçanes, where you'll find Celler de Capçanes – the big yellow building on your left as you enter the village. Established in 1933, this

USEFUL INFORMATION

Consell Regulador DO Montsant
Plaça Quartera 6
43730 Falset
Tel: +34 977 831 742
www.domontsant.com
info@domontsant.com

80-member-strong cooperative is most interesting for its unbelievably good kosher wine, Flor de Primavera. It's a blend of Cabernet Sauvignon, Garnacha, Cariñena, and Tempranillo, and if there's any left after the Jewish community in Barcelona has purchased its share, you'll find it on local wine lists at around 25 euros.

At both Celler de Capçanes and the next winery, Els Guiamets, you can buy olive oil, nuts, and local food products, as well as wine. Els Guiamets is still a rather dusty old *cooperativo*, but it did start bottling its own wine (as opposed to selling everything in bulk) five years ago. The top wine, Isis, is pretty impressive stuff and has an interesting label drawn by the artist Subirachs, but if you're just after super-cheap plonk you can pick up a 5-litre plastic flagon of Vi Blanc here for under 5 euros.

Set on Syrah

As you leave the village of Darmós travelling north, you'll find Joan d'Anguera signed off to the left. This pioneering bodega has always sought to establish a unique identity for Montsant, rather than letting it be seen as Priorat's second label. Josep Anguera Beyme, whose sons now run the estate, was also one of the first people to plant Syrah in Spain (in 1980), and this has been a continuing passion and point of difference for the company.

In El Masroig we're back with the cooperative movement and the Cooperativa Agrícola Sant Bartomeu, established in 1917. You can visit the winery 9am–1pm and 3–7pm on weekdays and there's a shop which sells oil, olives, *mistela* (unfermented grape juice with 60% brandy added to it), and wine. Throughout the region you'll occasionally come across old olive grinders being used as decoration and here there's one in the car park, sitting prettily between two silver-green olive trees.

On the road from El Masroig to El Molar, Clos Berenguer is signed off to the right. It's quite a bumpy, steep track down to the bodega, so make sure you have an appointment before attempting it.

El Molar

If you'd like to break up the route and spend a night in a sleepy little village, Perxe is a beautifully restored old house in the heart of El Molar, and a double room will cost you around 60 euros. As you leave the village and head east towards Falset, you're back in Priorat and you'll find La Perla del Priorat a little way along this road at Mas dels Frares. It's signed from the road and is also detailed on the information map in El Molar.

Seeing red

As you drive the road from El Molar to Bellmunt there's a sight not to be missed. It's as if some geologist desperate to reveal

WHERE TO STAY

Ca l'Aleixa [A/B4]
C/Major 19
43372 La Bisbal de Falset
Tel: +34 977 819 298
www.calaleixa.com

Cal Molí Barceló [C4]
Ricard Piqué 17
43775 Marçà
Tel: +34 977 830 515
calmolibarcelo@terra.es

Hostal Sport [B/C4]
Miquel Barceló 4–6
43730 Falset
Tel: +34 977 830 078
www.hostalsport.com

La Vinya del Pare [C4]
L'Hort de la Mare
43775 Marçà
Tel: +34 977 178 346
www.mothersgarden.org

L'Era (rural *gîte* sleeps 4)
[C4] C/del Barri 22
43774 La Torre de Fontaubella
Tel: +34 620 475 610
www.l-era.com

Perxe [B4]
43736 El Molar
Tel: +34 670 544 420
www.perxe.com

Montsant's unique soil structure had taken a giant knife and sliced straight through the earth, thereby exposing the distinct line between the chorizo-red sub-soil and its limestone coating.

The last stop on this route is the estate of Mas d'en Gil, again in Priorat, at Bellmunt del Priorat. As you enter the village you'll see the ghostly Museu de les Mines de Bellmunt del Priorat. Built around 1900, these lead mines were abandoned in 1972 and today, amongst other things, you can descend onto and explore the first-floor galleries of Mine Eugènia. Ask in Falset's tourist office about visiting arrangements.

At the far end of the village is the road off to Mas d'en Gil, and the short drive up to the old house through neatly tended vines and smart signposts is a visible indication of the substantial recent investment in the estate by the Rovira family. Originally known as Masia Barril, the company was established back in 1931, but it's only since the arrival of its new owners in 1998 that major changes have taken place. The old house has been substantially renovated, more land has been acquired and a smart new winery has been built, all with a view to becoming one of Priorat's elite.

BODEGAS IN MONTSANT

Agrícola Falset-Marçà [B/C4] Miquel Barceló 31
43730 Falset
Tel: +34 977 830 105
www.falsetmarca.com

Capafons-Ossó [B/C4]
Finca Maria Esplanes
43730 Falset
Tel: +34 977 831 201
www.capafons-osso.com

Celler de Capçanes [C4]
Llaberia 4
43776 Capçanes
Tel: +34 977 178 319
www.cellercapcanes.com

Cellers Joan d'Anguera [C4] Major 29
43746 Darmós
Tel: +34 977 418 348
anguerabeyme@teleline.es

Clos Berenguer [B/C4]
Ctra El Masroig – El Molar
43735 El Molar
Tel: +34 977 361 390
www.closberenguer.com

Cooperativa Agrícola Sant Bartomeu [C4]
Passeig de l'Arbre 3
43736 El Masroig
Tel: +34 977 825 050

Els Guiamets [C4]
C/Església 1
43777 Els Guiamets
Tel: +34 977 413 018

La Perla del Priorat [B4]
Mas dels Frares
43736 El Molar
Tel: +34 977 825 202

Mas d'en Gil [B4]
43738 Bellmunt del Priorat
Tel: +34 977 830 192
www.masdengil.com

ABOVE LEFT *Irrigation is used only while new plants get going.*

LEFT *The co-op in Falset.*

Tarragona

The only alcoholic beverage that used to be associated with Tarragona was a drink called "Tarragona Ruby" – a sweet, fortified red wine, usually made from Garnacha, which is kept in wood for a minimum of 12 years and ultimately tastes similar to tawny port. Today it's known as "Tarragona Clásico", and although small amounts are still made, the modern wines of Tarragona are a world apart from what in its heyday was known as "poor man's port".

Affordable wines

Tarragona's landscape is flatter and less dramatic than those of Priorat and Montsant, and the wines produced here are certainly less starry. What you find, however, are highly quaffable everyday wines that offer unbeatable value for money.

The region is split into two winemaking sub-zones: Comarca Ribera d'Ebre and Comarca del Camp. The first lies to the west of Priorat and Montsant, in the valley of the river Ebro. The second (within which you'll find the route described below), spreads out in all directions from the coastal town of Tarragona.

And so to bed

There are two hotels that I can't recommend highly enough in this region, and the first is Hotel Passamaner in La Selva del Camp. This grand terracotta-coloured old *masía* (country house) was designed by the modernist architect Domènech I Montaner and dates back to 1922. It was a ruin when an architect from Lanzarote got his hands on it and transformed it into a five-star luxury hotel, complete with spa complex and helicopter landing pad. All of the rooms and suites are named after famous Catalan

BELOW *The cooperative cellar in Nulles is one of the finest examples of a modernist winery in Tarragona.*

USEFUL INFORMATION

Tourist Office
Carrer de Sant Joan 34
43201 Reus
Tel: +34 902 360 200
www.reus.net/turisme/
infoturisme@reus.net

A tour of Reus entitled "The Modernist Trail" is conducted in English daily at 6pm from July to September.

modernist architects, and the attention to detail is exceptional.

If you choose to dine in the hotel's restaurant, La Gigantea, you'll be treated to a culinary feast courtesy of head chef Joaquín Koerper, himself the owner of a two-star Michelin restaurant in Alicante. The wine list is concise but entirely Spanish (other than a couple of Champagnes) and the emphasis is on wines from the northeast of Spain.

A little less glitzy but equally delightful is Hotel Rural Les Vinyes, just outside Montferri in the roadside village of Vilardida. Manja and Josep, a Dutch/Catalan couple, spent two years of constant hard graft renovating this old farmhouse winery into one of the most welcoming small hotels you could ever hope to find.

One of the highlights here is to book a massage in the underground treatment room that was once a cement wine vat. There's also a small, glass-encased indoor pool for further relaxation, and bicycles are loaned free of charge if you'd like to do some energetic exploring of the surrounding vineyards. Manja can arrange just about anything for you, including a trip on a friend's boat. The food is simple, home-cooked fare and the wines come from the two closest villages of Rodonyà and Montferri. The rooms are individually designed and include two beautiful suites (one of which is called "the vineyard"), each with a private terrace where you can eat breakfast overlooking a sea of vines.

ABOVE *The essential home-grown partner for Spain's delicious seafood.*

Getting there

The simplest and fastest way to cover the 77km (48-mile) route from Barcelona airport to Rodonyà is via the C32 motorway. After approximately 50km (31 miles), exit towards Calafell and pick up the C31 towards El Vendrell. At El Vendrell take the C51 road east to Rodonyà. If you want to avoid tolls, take the national C31 to El Vendrell and then pick up the C51 to Rodonyà. You can fly to Reus rather than Barcelona if you'd prefer (*see* p.106).

Travelling around

Route summary The route (*see* p.105 for map) begins in Rodonyà, a small village to the northeast of the town of Tarragona. It begins by heading west via Montferri to Bràfim, Nulles, and La Secuita, before dropping down to Reus. It finishes a few kilometres north of the town at the stunning Hotel Passamaner, which is described above. The route is approximately 55km (34 miles).

Route: a modernist dream

Although you'll find modernist wineries and buildings throughout the whole of Catalonia, this route perhaps more than any other could be described as a true *modernista* pilgrimage. From the wineries in Bràfim and Nulles and the Montferri santuari, to Reus'

BODEGAS IN TARRAGONA

Cellers del Camp de Tarragona [B1/2]
Sant Cristòfel 29
43765 La Secuita
Tel: +34 977 611 382

De Muller [C2/3]
Camí Pedra Estela 34
43205 Reus
Tel: +34 977 756 265
www.demuller.es
Visits cost €6 and include a tasting of five wines.

Vins Padró [B1]
Avinguda de Catalunya
43812 Bràfim
(No available telephone number)

Vinya Janine [B1]
C/Anselm Clavé 1
43812 Rodonyà
Tel: +34 977 628 305/033
vjanine@tinet.org

WHERE TO STAY

Hotel Passamaner [B2]
Camí de la Serra 52
43470 La Selva del Camp
Tel: +34 977 766 333
www.maspassamaner.com
hotel@maspassamaner.com
Prices from €175 for
a double room.

Hotel Rural Les Vinyes
[A/B1] 43812 Vilardida
Montferri
Tarragona
Tel: +34 977 639 193
www.lesvinyes.com
info@lesvinyes.com
€90–120 for a double
room with breakfast.

La Trampa [B2]
Camí de la Trampa s/n
43470 La Selva del Camp
Tel: +34 977 844 591
www.maslatrampa.com
maslatrampa@telefonica.net
€50–70 for a double
room.

gaggle of Gaudí-inspired buildings and Hotel Passamaner, the route is packed with awe-inspiring gems that will delight any fan of Spain's most influential artistic movement. Most cooperative wineries here are open for tourist visits only at weekends, so try to plan your trip accordingly.

Beginning in Rodonyà, Vinya Janine is a small winery that conducts visits on Saturday and Sunday mornings only. You'll be offered a tasting and also the chance to buy wine and olive oil from a shop which is hidden above and behind the winery. There's a sign to Vinya Janine off the main road that passes by Rodonyà.

The *garagiste celler* of Salvador Batlle, Masia Puig Adoll, is also based here, and if you speak Spanish then Manja from Hotel Les Vinyes may be able to arrange a visit for you. If not, and you're staying at the hotel, make sure you order a bottle of the bodega's wine with dinner. It's rustic, highly individual stuff that's produced in tiny quantities – I shared bottle number 699 (of just 715) of the 2001 Ull de Llebre/Merlot blend on a recent visit, and it was a perfect match for home-made wild boar pâté.

On leaving Rodonyà head west and then drop down south to Montferri where you'll find the Santuari de Montserrat, designed in 1925 by the modernist architect Josep Maria Jujol i Gibert. Discovering this fairytale structure as the late afternoon sun was gently setting on the village of Montferri was undoubtedly the most exciting moment of my entire time spent researching this book. It's so unexpected and so indescribably beautiful. From the jelly-mould shaped pale stone outer walls, complete with terrifying iron creatures, to the vividly coloured, stained-glass-dappled interior, it's utterly magical.

You're here for the wine of course and in Montferri you'll find a little cava producer, Cava Vives Ambròs, next to the bell tower in the main square. Again this wine is on the list of Hotel Les Vinyes and I can highly recommend it if you're in the mood for fizz.

Head back up to the C51 and turn left, then left again down to Bràfim, the next stop on the route. Take the sign after the one to Bràfim north into the village and you'll immediately come across the local cooperative, whose brand is Puig Rodó. At the opposite, south entrance to the town is Vins Padrò with its extraordinary grape-clad gates.

A short distance away in Nulles is a modernist cooperative that was designed in 1919 by Cèsar Martinell – it's one of the most impressive examples of such winery architecture that you're likely to find.

Lazy lunch

A little further south in La Secuita, as you take the turning towards Perafort, you'll find Cellers del Camp de Tarragona and its restaurant Abbatis. The 12-euro lunch menu at Abbatis is great value as it includes wine, water, and bread, and the portions are substantial. The daily menu may include freshly steamed asparagus with creamy cheese sauce followed by a large pile of melt-in-the-mouth deep-fried calamaris, and a refreshing pudding of mango sorbet. The bread comes in the form of "make your own" *pan con tomate* (explained on p.32). The still wines offered are all from the Cellers del Camp winery and are called Gamez Alba, whilst the cava (a fizz which goes a long way to prove that good cava doesn't have to come from Penedès) is labelled Gran d'Abbatis. With lunch I'd recommend a chilled glass of the cherry-flavoured Trepat rosé.

Round and round Reus

From La Secuita cut across west via Perafort and La Pobla de Mafumet to Reus. I'm not going to pretend that negotiating Reus in a car is without its frustrations, but as long as you're not in a hurry (and you remember that the tourist office is closed between 1.30 and 4pm) you shouldn't find it too harrowing. As I mentioned earlier, Reus is known for its modernist buildings and the tourist office conducts summer tours at 6pm each day. There's also a large food market, the Mercat Central (8am–2pm Mon–Thu; 7.30am–2.30pm Fri; 7.30am–3pm Sat), just opposite the tourist office on Calle Sant Joan.

Just outside Reus, to the south, is Bodegas de Muller (www.demuller.es for map details). Established in 1851 by a Frenchman from Alsace, the estate centres on the beautiful old 12th-century Masia Valls. The company makes wine under the denominations of Tarragona, Priorat, and Terra Alta (a region to the southwest of Tarragona), but is most famous for its fortified Vino de Misa (communion wine), which is sold all over the world. The route finishes at La Selva del Camp and the Hotel Passamaner.

WHERE TO EAT

Cerveseria Fereteria [B/C2]
Plaça de la Farinera 10
43201 Reus
Tel: +34 977 340 326

Restaurant Abbatis [B1/2]
Sant Cristòfol 29
43765 La Secuita
Tel: +34 977 611 448

LEFT *Santa Creus no longer houses a religious community, making it the only monastery on the Cistercian Route (see p.99) that you can explore fully.*

BELOW *The coast at Sitges.*

Penedès

Penedès is without doubt the best known of Catalonia's wine regions and as such it offers endless possibilities for eager wine tourists. It's most famous for producing cava, but the still wines of the region shouldn't be overlooked as they're often excellent, and very good value for money.

Here, there, and everywhere

There is literally a bodega around every corner you turn in this part of Spain and I doubt you'll go for more than five minutes without passing one. The three routes I've suggested below cover many of the best producers in the region, both large and small, but I'm sure that you're going to discover several more with wonderful cellars for you to see and delicious wines for you to taste.

At the centre of the region lie Vilafranca del Penedès and Sant Sadurní d'Anoia, the two most important wine towns. Vilafranca del Penedès is the larger of the two and although it is worth a visit for its tourist office, wine museum, and Saturday market, it's not the most picturesque or welcoming of places and I'd suggest you base yourself somewhere more rural to get the most from your stay.

BELOW *These parabolic arches at Codorníu are typical of the modernist period.*

What is cava?

One of the most popular sparkling wines in the world today is cava, and whether you pronounce it "carve", as the English do, with equal emphasis on the second syllable, or like the Spanish, "ca-ba" with "a" as in apple and "b" instead of "v" (and more emphasis on the first syllable), there's no better aperitif to a hearty Catalan dinner than a *copa* of this crisp, cool fizz.

How cava is made

All cava must be made according to the traditional method used in Champagne, with the second, bubble-inducing, fermentation taking place in the bottle. The traditional white grape varieties used have become unofficially known as "the big three" and are Xarel-lo, Macabeo, and Parellada. However, Chardonnay has, in recent years, become a popular addition to the blend, giving elegance and fruit structure to many quality wines.

The minimum ageing for cava is nine months,

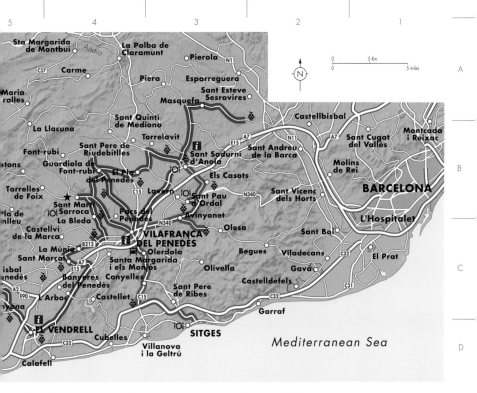

although *reservas* and *gran reservas* must be aged for considerably longer, and cava can be either a non-vintage or a vintage wine. Pink cava is also produced, usually from Monastrell or Garnacha.

Around 95% of all cava comes from the northeast of Spain and a great deal of the production centres around the town of Sant Sadurní d'Anoia. I could write reams about cava, but I'm going to stop now and leave you to discover the rest for yourself. Tip: Stick to the brut (dry) styles. The *semi-seco* (medium) ones don't have the elegance of *demi-sec* Champagne, and usually taste confected and sickly.

Route One: classic cava
45–50km (28–31 miles)

Route Two: the big boys
60km (37 miles)

Route Three: Vilafranca del Pènedes to La Bisbal
73km (45 miles)

Tale of Torres

If there's one company whose wines appear on virtually every restaurant list in Spain, it's Torres. This Catalan company, as I've already stated earlier in the book, has done more to modernize Spanish wines and winemaking than any other, and it continues to push the boundaries with a 3 million-euro annual budget for research and development.

Established in 1870, Torres is still a family-run company with fourth-generation Miguel A Torres firmly at the helm. He's supported by his daughter Mireia, who looks after the Research and Development Department, as well as production of the DO Catalunya Nerola wines, and his son Miguel Torres Jnr,

ABOVE *At Codorníu, Josep Puig i Cadafalch's "cathedral of cava" is as stunning today as it must have been when it was first designed over a century ago.*

RIGHT *The wines of Raventós i Blanc, both still and sparkling, are ideal for your next dinner party. The bottles look smart and the wine is equally good.*

USEFUL WEBSITES

www.agroturismealtpenedes.net
In Spanish, but has a link to a wine tourism site in English.

www.ecoturismecatalunya.com
If you speak Spanish this is good for finding interesting rural accomodation.

www.dopenedes.es

who's in charge of the Jean Leon winery and all marketing for the company.

On a visit here you'll learn about the colourful history behind the various Torres estates, and you'll also see the brand new cellar, which was still being built when I last visited. Tours include a glass of wine, and if you'd like to try others you can buy them by the glass – as long as you're not driving of course. As well as this main winery at Pacs del Penedès, Jean Leon at El Pla del Penedès, and vineyards in Conca de Barberà and Priorat, Torres also has projects as far afield as Chile, California, India, and China.

So what of the wines?

The Torres range is absolutely huge and I'm sure that if you like Spanish wines you'll already have tasted at least one of them. If you're not familiar with Mas La Plana you must try it. The Cabernet Sauvignon grapes for this single-vineyard wine are grown in front of Miguel Torres' own house, and the resulting wine is rich and concentrated with hints of wild herbs, coffee, and mint. It's Torres' top red and the one that really put the company on the fine wine map when the 1970 vintage beat Château Latour in the Paris Wine Olympiad of 1979. For light, aromatic summer drinking, Viña Esmeralda is consistently delicious and if you'd like to try one of the newer wines, the Nerola white or the new Priorat red are both extremely good. What Torres does best is to offer value for money at every level, so whatever your budget, I doubt you'll be disappointed.

Getting there

From Barcelona airport there are regular *cercanías* (suburban) trains to Vilafranca del Penedès via Sant Sadurní d'Anoia (www.renfe.es). If you choose to pick up a car at the airport, the drive is 58km (36 miles) on the A2 and A7 motorways to Vilafranca del Penedès. If you'd prefer to use the national road then head north from the airport and take a left to meet the N340 just past Sant Vicenç dels Horts.

Travelling around

As Penedès is packed with bodegas, there are three suggested routes. Each takes in a mixture of cava and still wine producers (many houses make both), although Route One has an emphasis on cava, and Route Two a stronger focus on the still wine producers.

Route One summary This route begins in true cava country just outside Sant Sadurní d'Anoia. From here head south, crossing the A7 motorway, to Els Casots and on down to pick up the N340 (national road). Turn right onto the N340 and right again up to Sant Pau d'Ordal before returning to the N340 and heading west to Avinyonet del Penedès. Drop down to Can Rafols and then back to the national road. Finally take the C15 to just outside Vilanova i la Geltrú and the C32 motorway for the short distance to Sitges. Approximately 45–50km (28–31 miles).

Route Two summary The second route begins northeast of Sant Sadurní d'Anoia just outside Sant Esteve Sesrovires. Head west and up past Masquefa and then drop down to the outskirts of Sant Sadurní d'Anoia before heading west in an anti-clockwise circle via Torrelavit, El Pla del Penedès, Guardiola de Font-rubi, Pacs del Penedès, and Vilafranca del Penedès. The route finishes just south of Sant Sadurní. This route is around 60km (37 miles).

Route Three summary The third route begins at Vallformosa, situated on the road north out of Vilafranca del Penedès towards Guardiola de Font-rubi. Continue north and then across west to Sant Martí Sarroca. After dropping down to La Bleda head west and south once again to Sant Marçal, before picking up the main N340 to El Vendrell. Finally take the C51 northwest to La Bisbal del Penedès and continue on to Vilardida. The route is 73km (45 miles), not including the small detour out of El Vendrell to Puig i Roca.

Route One: classic cava

If you'd like to see the difference between a huge cava company and a smaller, almost boutique-style producer, there's no better way than to visit both Codorníu and Raventós i Blanc. The reason I've selected these two is not only because they're excellent producers, but also because they're conveniently situated next door to one another. If you follow the signs from Sant Sadurní d'Anoia to Raventós, you'll be sure to find them both.

Codorníu's reception hall, which used to be the winery, is a beautiful old modernist building, "a cathedral of cava", designed by Josep Puig i Cadafalch at the end of the 19th century. Over 200,000 visitors pass through Codorníu's glamorous gates each year, and tours are free unless you choose to call in at the weekend, when you'll be charged 2 euros for your

BODEGAS IN PENEDES

Albet i Noya [B3]
Can Vendrell de la Codina
08739 Sant Pau d'Ordal
Tel: +34 938 994 812
www.albetinoya.com

Can Ràfols Dels Caus [C3]
08793 Avinyonet del Penedès
Tel: +34 637 817 644
www.canrafolsdelscaus.com

Cava Llopart [B3]
08739 Subirats
Tel: +34 938 993 125
www.llopart.es

Cava Rovellats [B/C4]
La Bleda
08731 Sant Martí Sarroca
Tel: +34 934 880 575
www.cavasrovellats.com

Codorníu [B3]
Avda Jaume Codorníu s/n
08770 Sant Sadurní d'Anoia
Tel: +34 938 913 342
www.codorniu.com

RIGHT *Codorníu's cava house.*

BELOW *Albet i Noya.*

tasting glass (which you can then keep). A tour lasts around an hour and a half and you'll be shown the cellar in which it's reputed the first ever bottle of cava was opened.

There is, in fact, a great deal of important cava history attached to Codorníu, as it was here that cava was first made on a commercial scale back in 1872 by Don José Raventós. Today this large company owns 11 wineries, one of which is in Argentina, and it also rents the Pinot Noir vineyard at the Monestir de Poblet in Conca de Barberà (see p.98). There's a lovely light and airy museum housed in the old press room, but if you want to see some action in the winery, then September and October are certainly the best months to plan your visit.

Jaume de Codorníu is the top wine, sold in magnums, of which only 10,000 are made each year. It's not widely available for obvious reasons, but you can buy it here if you've got 50 euros to spare. Codorníu is well known for its (initially controversial) use of the Champagne grapes Chardonnay and Pinot Noir in its cavas. I'd suggest you try Anna de Codorníu (70% Chardonnay with Parellada and Macabeo) and then compare the taste sensation with other cavas made exclusively from the three traditional grape varieties.

Raventós i Blanc is linked to Codorníu, as it was established (in 1986) by part of the same family. (Tours here are conducted 9am–5pm, Mon–Fri). It is, however, a much smaller operation than its neighbour and you won't find anyone to show you around in August (when everyone is on holiday) or during the September harvest, when picking and pressing understandably have to take priority over visitors. I've always loved the stylish packaging of the Raventós wines, and what's inside the bottle is usually pretty good too. Try the L'Hereu Brut cava and the delicious La Rosa Merlot rosé still wine.

Small and organic

From Sant Sadurní d'Anoia take the BP2427 south past Els Casots and Cava Llopart, (there's also a farm offering olive oil tastings on this road) to the main N340 national road. Turn right and then right again up to Sant Pau d'Ordal where you might like to stop for lunch at restaurant Cal Xim. I'm going to be completely honest and admit I haven't tried it myself, but it does come highly and reliably recommended.

On the way you'll have passed Albet i Noya and it's now time to retrace your steps and pay a visit. In 1979 Josep Albet i Noya's family bought the property they'd run for almost 100 years. Being a vegetarian, he wanted to farm in an environmentally friendly way and the vineyards of Albet i Noya are today managed organically. This doesn't, of course, guarantee better-tasting wine, but it's good for the environment and good for you – especially if you're prone to allergies, as the level of sulphur in the wines is lower than normal. The winery produces both sparkling and still wines, and the Cava Brut 21 NV is one of the best cavas I've tasted. You could also try Núria, named after Josep's mother, a creamy blend of Merlot with the rarely seen Caladoc and Arinarnoa grape varieties.

Still wines and sandy beaches
Head west to Avinyonet del Penedès, take the sign to Olesa, and after a couple of kilometres (about a mile) you'll come to Can Ràfols dels Caus. This beautiful old *masía* is situated in hilly terrain on the borders of the Garraf National Park. The soil and bedrock here are predominantly calcareous, part of a geological formation that stretches across the National Park to the coast, and one which sets this area apart from the rest of Penedès. With its French grape varieties and steely, structured wines, Can Ràfols seems almost like a mini-Bordeaux and the wines it produces are certainly more suited to ageing than most you'll find in Penedès. The Gran Caus, a typical Bordeaux blend of Cabernet Franc, Cabernet Sauvignon, and Merlot, is superb. For interest's sake, try the Vinya el Rocalis made from 100% Incroccio Manzoni, a virtually unknown Riesling/Pinot Blanc cross.

From here pick up the N340 west again and then drop down on the C15 towards Vilanova i la Geltrú. At the junction with the main C32 motorway there's a Rutas del Vino y del Cava sign directing you to Jaume Serra, a bodega with a view of the Mediterranean.

Your final stop is the coastal town of Sitges, perhaps better known for its gay scene than its wines, but always a fun place to spend a night. Restaurant Alfresco is the place to eat and, if they're in season when you visit, you must try the baked figs stuffed with creamy white cheese and wrapped in wafer-thin Serrano ham.

Route Two: the big boys
This route has more of an emphasis on the still wines of Penedès and takes in wineries belonging to three of its major companies; Torres, Codorníu, and Freixenet. Just outside Sant Esteve Sesrovires you'll find Masia Bach, owned by the Codorníu group mentioned in Route One. The history of the company dates back to 1915 when two brothers from Barcelona invested the profits from their cotton business in a winery, and subsequently presented their first wines at the Barcelona Trade Fair in 1929. After several changes of ownership, the estate was finally acquired by Codorníu, which

BODEGAS IN PENEDES (CONTINUED)

Jané Ventura [D5]
Ctra de Calafell 2
43700 El Vendrell
Tel: +34 977 660 118
www.janeventura.com

Jean Leon [B3/4]
Pago Jean Leon 40
08775 Torrelavit
Tel: +34 938 995 512
www.jeanleon.com

Joan Sardá [C4]
Ctra Vilafranca –
Sant Jaume 8.1km
08732 Castellví de la Marca
Tel: +34 938 918 053

Masia Bach [A2]
Ctra Martorell –
Capellades 20.5km
08635 Sant Esteva Sesrovires
Tel: +34 937 714 052
www.grupocodorniu.com

Miguel Torres [B/C4]
Finca el Maset
08796 Pacs del Penedès
Tel: +34 938 177 487
www.torreswines.com

continued over the page

BODEGAS IN PENEDES (CONTINUED)

Mont Marçal [C4]
Finca Manlleu
08732 Castellvi de
la Marça
Tel: +34 938 918 281
itort@mont-marcal.com

Puig i Roca [D5]
(signed Celler Augustus Forum)
Ctra de Sant Vicenç
43700 El Vendrell
Tel: +34 977 666 910

Raventós i Blanc [B3]
Plaça del Roure
08770 Sant Sadurní
d'Anoia
Tel: +34 938 183 262
www.raventos.com

Segura Viudas [B3]
Ctra Sant Pere
Riudebitlles 5km
08775 Torrelavit
Tel: +34 938 917 070
www.seguraviudas.es

Vallformosa [B4]
La Sala 45
08735 Vilobí del Penedès
Tel: +34 938 978 286
www.vallformosa.es

BELOW *200,000 visitors
enter these gates each year.*

in 1988 employed architect Domingo Triay to sensitively update and extend the original Tuscan/Spanish country house winery. A wide range of still wines and cavas is produced today, with the unoaked Masia Bach Chardonnay representing a typical modern Penedès white, offering value for money at around 5 euros.

From here continue on the B224 past Masquefa and then drop down the BV 2241 towards Sant Sadurní d'Anoia. Take a right towards Sant Pere de Riudebitlles and you'll find the next winery along this road. Although now owned by Freixenet, Segura Viudas still operates independently and produces a wide range of cavas and still wines from its home, a former lookout tower that dates back to the 11th century.

Time for Torres: Jean Leon

To reach Jean Leon at El Pla del Penedès you'll need to take a left on the BV 2153. This company is now part of the Torres empire, but the name of its founder Jean Leon is still an important part of the brand. Spanish-born Leon was most famous for playing host to Hollywood's glitterati at his La Scala restaurant, before he decided to turn his hand to winemaking at the beginning of the 1960s. Jean Leon now has an impressive new visitor's centre, and a tour will include a short video detailing the main man's life, a visit to the museum, the winery, the vineyards and the cellars, and a tasting of two wines (cost: 3 euros).

Although you may not be offered it to taste on your tour, the relatively new top wine, Jean Leon Zemis, is elegant, stylish, and definitely worth buying. A blend of Cabernet Sauvignon, Merlot, and Cabernet Franc, it displays structured blackcurrant fruit along with notes of bell pepper and cedar wood. For a deliciously fresh and aromatic white, on the other hand, try the Terrasola Muscat/Parellada, a wine that falls perfectly between the styles of Viña Sol and

ABOVE *The beach at Sitges.*

Viña Esmeralda – two extremely popular and eminently drinkable Torres stalwarts.

Head west from here to Guardiola de Font-rubi and then drop down on the BV2127 to Pacs dels Penedès and the unmissable Torres estate and winery. This book is, in many ways, about seeking out small producers and unknown wines, as opposed to large companies with impressive visitor centres. It is, however, impossible to really understand Penedès (or modern Spanish wines in the case of Torres) without taking a look at wineries such as this and Codorníu. I've talked a lot about Torres already, so all I'll add is that visits here are free, and on my last visit the Tunnel of the Seasons was the newest attraction and a Garden of the Senses was being planned. The shop has a touch-screen computer with details of every wine sold, and the prices are slightly more attractive than they would be at home.

Sun, vines, and sleep time

Drop down to Vilafranca del Penedès and take the C243 towards Sant Sadurní d'Anoia. Just before you reach the town you'll come across Hotel Sol i Vi, sitting by the side of the road on your right. The name alone ("Sun and Wine") manages to capture the essence of Catalonia in three simple words, and although the bedrooms are basic, there's an open-air swimming pool and a very long wine list. One or

ADDITIONAL BODEGAS

Agusti Torelló
(Sant Sadurní d'Anoia)
Tel: +34 938 911 173
www.agustitorello.com

Alemany i Corrio
(Vilafranca del Penedès)
Tel: +34 938 172 587
sotlefriec@totpenedes.com

Can Feixes (Huguet)
(Vilafranca del Penedès)
Tel: +34 937 718 227
www.canfeixes.com

Covides
(Sant Sadurní d'Anoia)
Tel: +34 938 911 061
www.covides.com

continued on p.131

two specific moments made me like this place more than I might otherwise have done, and the first was when they told me I could drink my own wines with dinner. Not only that, the waiter also graciously decanted them for me before taking a big felt marker pen and writing the name of each wine on the side of its decanter. Another treat was to have a whole leg of Serrano ham brought to my dinner table and expertly carved in front of me. And finally on this particular Tuesday evening, just as I was finishing dessert and starting to contemplate the comfort of my bed, I witnessed the most endearing incident of all – an elderly Spanish couple were warmly welcomed as they strolled nonchalantly in for dinner at 11.15pm.

In the restaurant you can choose from set menus at 12 and 24 euros, as well as the *à la carte* menu, and the extensive wine list offers everything from basic cava at 12 euros to a full complement of the Bordeaux first growths.

Route Three:
Vilafranca del Penedès to La Bisbal

This route begins in the Alt Penedès just north of Vilafranca, and moves west into the Baix Penedès, the part of the region that is furthest south from Barcelona.

Vallformosa is situated on the BV2127 from Vilafranca to Guardiola. This estate, owned by the Domenech family since 1865, has grown enormously in recent years and has developed from its status as a supplier of base wine for cava into a major producer of sparkling and still wines in its own right. The large modern winery building is where most of the work is done and new visitor facilities are under construction as I write, but if you'd like to see one of the family's beautiful old *masias*, stop off towards the end of the route at La Bisbal del Penedès. Follow the signs out of the town to the cemetery and you'll see Masia Finca Freyé on the left, just after the cemetery and next door to Finca Mas Vilella, which belongs to Jané Ventura (mentioned later). Masia Finca Freyé is stunning, with landscaped gardens that feature huge old *tinajas* (similar to a large earthenware vase and used many years ago for storing wine) sitting decoratively amongst flowers and vines.

Time for church

From Vallformosa continue on up to Guardiola de Font-rubi and then turn left onto the BV2151 to Sant Martí Sarroca. The town itself is rather unremarkable, but the church and

WHERE TO EAT

Al Fresco [D3]
Pau Barrabeitg 4
08870 Sitges
Tel: +34 938 940 600

Cal Lluís 1887 [B4]
C/de la Font 32–34
08731 Sant Martí Sarroca
Tel: +34 938 991 001

Cal Manescal [B4]
C/Ferran Muñoz
Gasco 10
08731 Sant Martí Sarroca
Tel: +34 938 991 358

Cal Xim [B3]
Plaça Subirats 5
Sant Pau d'Ordal
08739 Barcelona
Tel: +34 938 993 092
www.calxim.com

Castell de Sant Martí are beautiful, perched as they are on a hill overlooking the surrounding vine-clad countryside. As you take the winding road up from Sant Martí you'll pass a couple of well-situated restaurants where you might like to stop for lunch and a well-deserved rest.

Cava Rovellats at La Bleda is next on the itinerary. As you drop down from Sant Martí towards Vilafranca, don't take the first road off to the right signed La Bleda, take the second which has a sign to the bodega itself. (Be warned, the map on the website is confusing.) This is a family company whose emphasis is on the artisanal production of quality cavas (although it does also produce some still wine), made exclusively from its own grapes and aged for a minimum of two years. At the centre of this 210ha estate sits the old 15th-century *masia*, complete with chapel and modernist gardens. For a visit that sums up traditional cava production, albeit with a little Chardonnay thrown in for good measure, you couldn't be in a better place.

A hidden gem

Drop down from La Bleda to the B212 and turn right towards La Munia. Shortly after the town you'll pass on your right Bodegas Joan Sardá, which produces mostly still wines. In order to find the next winery you'll almost certainly need to contact the bodega for directions. Mont Marçal is situated above the town of Sant Marçal and is tricky to find, but call them and a lovely lady called Iolanda will send you directions. Visits are usually conducted in the morning and conclude with a glass of cava. There's also a small shop, and of the wines I've tasted recently, the Mont Marçal Blanc and the Mont Marçal Rosé are both lovely examples of fresh, modern Penedès wines.

Still and sparkling

Jané Ventura is situated in the town of El Vendrell (you need to take the N340 southwest from just below Sant Marçal). The first thing I'd suggest you do when you arrive is to head straight for the centre of town and the tourist office, where you can ask for directions to Jané Ventura and pick up a map of the local area which details the Puig i Roca winery. Jané Ventura is on the east side of town, near the railway tracks and opposite the police station. It's a practical, sand-coloured building which is open from Monday to Saturday for visits, and sells both wine and cava under the

LEFT *The famous Torres winery.*

BELOW *The vineyard at Jean Leon, one of Torres' newest acquisitions.*

USEFUL INFORMATION
. . . .
Tourist Office El Vendrell
Avda Brisamar 1
43880 El Vendrell
Tel: +34 977 680 010
www.elvendrell.net or
www.elvendrellturistic.com

Tourist Office Sant Sadurní d'Anoia
Plaça Ajuntament 1
08770 Sant Sadurní d'Anoia
Tel: +34 938 910 325
www.santsadurni.org

Tourist Office Subirats
Estació Vitivinícola
(Renfe Estación)
08739 Lavern (Subirats)
Tel: +34 938 993 499
www.turismesubirats.com
This site has wine routes.

Tourist Office Vilafranca
C/de la Cort 14
08720 Vilafranca del Penedès
Tel: +34 938 920 358
www.ajvilafranca.es

Turisme Alt Penedès
Hermenegild Clascar 1–3
08720 Vilafranca del Penedès
Tel: +34 938 900 000
www.altpenedes.net

Turisme Vilafranca
C/de la Fruita 13
08720 Vilafranca del Penedès
Tel: +34 938 181 254
www.turismevilafranca.com

Jané Ventura and Finca Els Camps brands. The 16th-century house and vineyard Mas Vilella at La Bisbal del Penedès (*see* Vallformosa p.130) is a far more attractive sight, however, and it's sometimes possible to arrange a visit and tasting there as well as in El Vendrell.

Before heading up the C51 to La Bisbal del Penedès, a small detour via Puig i Roca is called for. Follow the signs out of El Vendrell towards St Vicenç de Calders. When you reach a fork in the road take a left and shortly afterwards you'll see a sign to Celler Augustus Forum. The wines and the vineyards have both been given Roman names, as the old Via Augusta (Roman road) used to run right past the estate. Augustus is a small range of top-quality, limited-production wines made from international grape varieties, and is complemented by a couple of gourmet wine vinegars available under the Forum label. If you ring for a visit ask for Albert Roca, who speaks English.

Other things to do
Vilafranca's wine museum has evidence that vines were in existence in Penedès before the 4th century BC – that evidence comes in the form of two press plates that were found during the excavation of a couple of ancient villages in the region.

Penedès wine facts
In terms of wine-growing areas the region is split into three sub-zones: the Alt Penedès, which is the furthest from the sea, the highest, and, due to its cooler nights, the one most suited to delicate, aromatic grape varieties; the Mitja Penedès, which is heavily planted with the traditional cava grapes mentioned below; and the Baix (low) Penedès, which is the closest to the sea and tends to have plantings of mostly indigenous red varieties and cava grapes.

The latest figures show that the region has 27,730ha of vines and currently produces around 47 million bottles of wine a year. Not surprisingly, the most widely planted grape variety is Xarel-lo, closely followed by its cava partners, Macabeo and Parellada.

Rutas del vino y del cava
There are seven of these routes (*see* www.enoturismealtpenedes.net) which are signposted throughout the region, and there's even a special tourist bus that follows one of them. If you'd like to know more just ask in Vilafranca's tourist office for a map.

JEAN LEON

Empordà-Costa Brava

The Empordà-Costa Brava is a wild and beautiful place, and whether you choose to visit its wineries, bathe in its wine (more of this anon), eat freshly landed fish or just lie by the sea, you can't help but be captivated by its rugged charm.

Neighbours with France

The region (Ampurdán-Costa Brava in Castilian) nestles snugly against the border with France, just a stone's throw away from Roussillon, and is Catalonia's most northerly wine DO. Its rugged, precipitous green landscape is very similar to that of its neighbour, yet Empurdà's wines have traditionally been quite different. Other than a certain similarity between its heady sweet wines and those of Banyuls, Empurdà has always been considered to be a producer of run-of-the-mill rosé, whilst the sun-kissed vineyards of southern France are far better known for yielding chunky, full-bodied reds.

In the past few years, however, all this has begun to change, as new experimental plantings of Cabernet Sauvignon, Syrah, and Merlot for the reds, and Chardonnay and Chenin for the whites, have led to the production of some fascinating new wines.

Other than Castillo Perelada, a large company which dominates production, you'll find cooperatives and small, family-run businesses making most of the wine. The climate is Mediterranean, and although the cold Tramontana wind that blows fiercely from the north does help the grapes to keep their cool, careful vineyard site selection and management are vital if wind damage is to be avoided.

Ancient Empúries

As you travel from Barcelona or Girona to the Empordà-Costa Brava, there's one detour that's well worth making. This is a visit to the ancient Greco-Roman archaeological site of Empúries. The Greeks first settled here in the 6th century BC, at a time when trade with the Iberian peninsula was becoming a popular and lucrative business. The settlement of Emporion (which means "trade" in ancient Greek) was founded shortly afterwards and with it came the beginnings of local Iberian culture.

In 218 BC the Romans arrived and built their own, rather larger, settlement complete with amphitheatre, elegant villas, and sophisticated water purification system. During the reign

BIG PLANS FOR PERELADA

In 2007 **Castillo Perelada** (a short drive northeast of Figueres) will open the doors to its **impressive new 12 million euro winery**, which is currently under construction. The new structure will incorporate a series of existing farm buildings which will be transformed into a reception area and visitor centre. Current production will double and between **50,000 and 100,000 visitors** are expected each year to view the whole winemaking process from a hanging walkway.

LEFT *The new visitor centre at Jean Leon.*

BELOW *Stone walls at Capmany.*

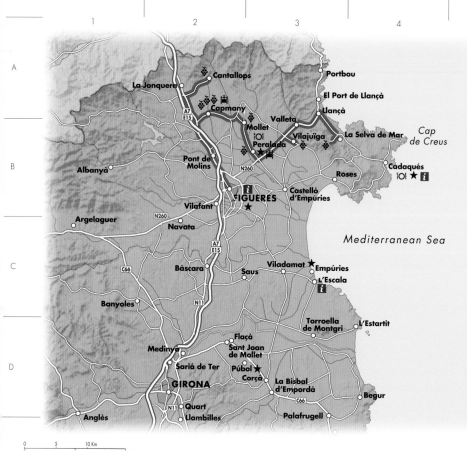

0 5 10 Km
0 5 10 miles

N

Route: Cadaqués

of Emperor Augustus, the Greek and Roman cities were united under the title Municipium Emporiae and the Romanization of Spain had begun.

What's interesting to wine lovers, of course, is to know what wine these people were drinking, or indeed if they were drinking wine at all. The answer lies in the archaeology museum at Empúries, where you'll find an erotic drinking vessel that was dug from the site.

Follow signs to Ruines d'Empúries – tickets cost 2.40 euros and include entrance to the museum. There's free parking close to the sight and a small beach if you fancy taking a dip.

Getting there

The Empordà-Costa Brava can be reached most easily by flying to either Girona or Perpignan (in France) – Ryanair (www.ryanair.com) offers cheap flights to both, although only from Stansted in the case of Perpignan. Car hire is available at both airports.

From Girona take either the A7/E15 motorway or the N11 national road north to beyond Figueres (coming off at Junction 2 towards La Jonquera if using the motorway), and then pick up the GI601 east to Cantallops (approximately 64km/40 miles). From Perpignan, again take either the main motorway or national road south, and again pick up the GI601 east (approximately 51km/31.5 miles).

ABOVE *This Greco-Roman archaeological site at Empúries dates back to the 6th century BC.*

Travelling around
Route summary and alternatives In summertime the last 30 minutes of the journey east along the road to Cadaqués from Figueres is breathtaking. Abandoned terraces cling resolutely to the steep, sunbaked slopes, whilst silver green olive and almond trees pave the winding way to the sea. Although my suggested route doesn't include this road, an alternative idea would be to drive straight from Girona, via Figueres, to Cadaqués for an overnight stop, and then begin the route in reverse the following day. If you choose this option and have enough time, try to visit Empúries on the way up. It is a bit of a detour as it's situated on the coast halfway between Girona and Figueres, but it really is worth the effort.

It's very tempting not to mention Cadaqués at all for fear of spoiling this lovely little seaside town by adding to the hordes of visitors already familiar with its charms – but on consideration it would be unfair not to include one of my very favourite summer destinations. With its whitewashed buildings, narrow cobbled streets, gently bobbing boats, and small seafront restaurants, it's one of the most delightful places on the whole of the northeast coast.

Hotel Playa Sol offers the perfect combination of being situated right beside the sea in the heart of the town, yet with a secluded open-air pool and restaurant area to the rear. For dinner, restaurant Es Baluard is on the opposite side of the bay and has open picture windows with views out to sea. It also serves a very tasty *paella* that goes extremely well with a bottle of chilled Enate rosé (see Somontano chapter, p.85).

Route: Cadaqués
The route proper begins in Cantallops, directly north of Figueres. Masia Serra is one of the family-run businesses alluded to earlier, and the 12ha estate was planted back in 1961 by Simón Serra's grandfather. Initially the grapes were sold off to other companies but now Masia Serra makes its own wines, all with very specific names. The white Ctònia, for example, is named after a character from Greek

WHERE TO EAT

Es Baluard [B4]
17488 Cadaqués
Tel: +34 972 258 183

El Bulli [B3]
Cala Montjoi Ap 30
17480 Roses
Tel: +34 972 150 457
www.elbulli.com
You'll need to book months
and months in advance
to eat at Ferran Adrià's
legendary restuarant
(see p.139).

ABOVE RIGHT *A brand new
12 million-euro, state-of-the-art
winery is currently being built at
the stunning Castillo Perelada.*

BELOW *If you've dreamt of
buying a vineyard and working
it yourself, visit Mas Estela to
see first-hand the heartaches
and the highs of such a venture.*

mythology who was linked with the earth and the underworld, symbolizing the depth to which the Garnacha Blanca vine roots reach. For interest you should also try the Ino, a *solera* system (which is normally used in sherry production), sweet, oxidized-style wine that draws from a "mother" barrel dating back to 1860 – hence the name Ino, Dionysus' aunt, and his mother Semele's sister.

Around Capmany

From Cantallops take the GI601 back to the main N11 and head south. Turn left onto the GI602 towards Mollet and stop off at Capmany. The town has three good wineries, the first of which is Oliveda. Here, along with a wide range of wines and cavas, you'll find a museum of wine taps (open 9am–1pm, 3–6pm, except Sundays and holidays).

Pere Guardiola (which isn't open to visitors) and Oliver Conti are the two other recommended bodegas in Capmany, with the latter having been established from scratch as recently as 1991. From the outset its creators wanted to innovate and decided against planting the traditional Garnacha and Cariñena of the region. Instead they chose Cabernet Sauvignon, Merlot, Cabernet Franc, Gewürztraminer, and Sauvignon Blanc, as well as some experimental Pinot Noir, Touriga Nacional, Viognier, and Marsanne. The winery building is state of the art and the company is one to watch.

A little further down the road in Mollet is Vinícola del Nordest, a joint venture between the Mollet cooperative and Cavas del Ampurdán (part of the Castillo Perelada estate). The winery is open for visits (9am–1pm and 3–7pm, Mon–Fri) and there's also a small shop where you can buy any one of the extensive range of wines and cavas, as well as the company's own olive oil.

Museum, wine cellar, and library

Castillo Perelada is by far the largest company in the region and well worth a visit for many different reasons. The company's wine shop La Botiga de Celler (where visits usually begin) is located in the centre of town. Just opposite is the magnificent 14th-century castle which contains a casino and a restaurant. There's also an adjoining monastery with a museum, a wine cellar from 1923, and a library with over 80,000 volumes – 1,000 of which are editions of *Don Quixote De La Mancha* (the classic early-17th-century novel by Miguel de Cervantes) in 30 different languages.

You'll find all the Perelada range available to buy in the shop, along with a selection of Spanish and international wines. The top wine, Gran Claustro, is a blend of Cabernet Sauvignon and Merlot, and although it's expensive, having

tasted the last couple of vintages I highly recommend that you invest in a bottle or two. There are various different options to choose from in terms of visits, all of which include a tour of the castle's museum and a glass of cava (prices range from 5–7 euros for visits, with additional wine tasting costing from 3–5 euros per person).

Wine spa and relaxation

It's best to visit in July and August when the weather is good and the summer festival is in full swing (*see* below). If you can afford to treat yourself (especially if you're a golfer – green fees are 35–51 euros), then the Golf Perelada is a five-star hotel with a wine spa. Treatments include such luxuries as exfoliation with grape seeds (45 euros) and bathing in Merlot or Muscat (31 euros).

Crazy labels

From Perelada (note: some maps spell it Peralada) drop down to the N260 and then head towards the coast before turning right onto the G1610. The left turning to Celler Espelt is just after the one to Vilajuïga. This state-of-the-art winery cultivates no less than 17 different grape varieties which are made into white, red, rosé, sweet, and sparkling wines. The most appealing thing here though is the design of the labels, which manage to capture beautifully the carefree, sunny, Mediterranean feel of the region.

Biodynamic winery

The last stop on this route is at Mas Estela in La Selva de Mar. Take the N260 east again and head for Llança. From here pick up the G1612 down to La Selva de Mar. Mas Estela is tucked away up a dirt track and is virtually impossible to find without assistance, but ask any of the locals and they'll point you in the right direction.

BODEGAS IN
EMPORDA-COSTA BRAVA

Castillo Perelada [B3]
Plaça del Carme 1
17491 Perelada
Tel: +34 932 233 022
www.perelada.com

Celler Espelt [B3]
Paratge Mas Satlle s/n
17493 Vilajuïga
Tel: +34 972 531 727
www.cellerespelt.com

Mas Estela [A2]
17489 La Selva de Mar
Tel: +34 972 126 176
masestela@hotmail.com

Masia Serra [A2]
C/Dels Solés 20
17708 Cantallops
Tel: +34 629 335 022
gestec@tiservinet.es

Oliveda [A2]
C/La Roca 3
17750 Capmany
Tel: +34 972 549 012
www.grupoliveda.com

Oliver Conti [A2]
C/Puignau
17750 Capmany
Tel: +34 972 193 161
www.oliverconti.com

Vinícola del Nordest [A3]
Carrer d'Espolla 9
17752 Mollet de Perelada
Tel: +34 972 563 150
www.vinicola
delnordest.com

For the past 18 years a wonderful couple (Didier and Nuria) have owned and farmed this 14ha estate with the help of their three sons. They've always worked the land according to organic principles and have recently started to convert to Biodynamics. They produce their own electricity, and water for irrigation is collected in tanks positioned on top of the mountains.

When the couple first saw this crumbling old house and vineyard all those years ago, they fell in love with it because, as Nuria says, "it felt so close to the stars". It's a truly beautiful place and if you'd like to spend some time getting back to nature and breathing fresh, vine-scented mountain air, you can ask Nuria about renting out the winery's little guest cottage for a few days.

Mas Estela produces around 40,000 bottles a year of mostly red wine, although there is a small amount of white and sweet Muscat made too. The rich and heady reds contain a classic Mediterranean mix of Grenache, Mourvèdre, Syrah, and Cariñena, whilst the equally punchy white is a blend of Chardonnay and Muscat.

Cap de Creus

As you're so close, after visiting Mas Estela, it would be a great pity not to go and stand on the most easterly tip of the Iberian peninsula, the Cap de Creus. With its stunning views of the rugged coastline it's reputedly best at dawn and sunset. To get there take the GI613 east from La Selva de Mar.

Dalliance with Dalí

Catalonia is well known for having produced more than its fair share of talented artists over the years, with Gaudí and Miró being native to the region and Picasso, though born in Málaga, having spent most of his formative years in Barcelona. Once you cross the invisible boundary into Figueres and beyond, however, there's one man whose name and work you simply can't avoid. It is of course the mustachioed, bohemian, and ever so slightly bonkers, Surrealist painter Salvador Dalí.

There are three major stops for Dalí fans in this area and the first is his museum in Figueres. Created by the artist himself in the early 1970s on the site of an old theatre, this most bizarre of buildings, topped with enormous cream eggs, houses the widest range of his work to be found anywhere. The second is the medieval castle of Púbol to the east of Girona, originally the home of Dalí's wife Gala and today the Gala Dalí Castle museum-house.

Soon after World War II, Dalí and Gala moved to Port Lligat (just north of Cadaqués) and it's here that you'll find the third Dalí museum, the couple's highly individual former home. Due to its size visitor numbers are restricted and it's necessary to book in advance.

El Bulli

It would be impossible to talk to wine-lovers about this area without mentioning Ferran Adrià's world-famous El Bulli restaurant, situated just 7km (just over 4 miles) from Roses at Cala Montjoi. For over 20 years this extraordinary chef has been creating weird and wonderful culinary concoctions that have occasionally shocked, almost always surprised, and frequently delighted his eager guests. Indeed his fame is such that it's become virtually impossible to secure a table unless you ring the moment the booking lines open at the beginning of the year. The restaurant opens (evenings only) from April until September and is closed on Mondays and Tuesdays during April, May, and June.

Festivities in Perelada

During July and August, Perelada springs to life with its Festival Castell de Perelada, a music festival now in its twentieth year. The festival takes place in the grounds of the stunning castle and includes everything from opera and dance to Latin jazz, performed in a series of over 20 concerts. Most shows begin at either 9pm or 10pm, allowing the audience plenty of time to make the most of the open-air buffet supper offered by Restaurant La Parrilla dels Jardins (tel: +34 972 538 292), which costs around 40 euros per person.

ADDITIONAL INFORMATION

The Archaeological Museum of Catalonia [C3]
17130 Empúries
L'Escala
Tel: +34 972 770 208
macempuries.cultura
@gencat.net

Teatre-Museu Dalí [B2]
Plaça Gala i Salvador Dalí 5
17600 Figueres
Tel: +34 972 677 500/9
www.dali-estate.org
t-mgrups@dali-estate.org for the Figueres museum
pllgrups@dali-estate.org for the house at Port Lligat
pbgrups@dali-estate.org for the castle at Púbol

www.cbrava.com
This site offers useful general information on the region.

LEFT *The ruggedly beautiful Cap de Creus lies a few kilometres east of La Selva de Mar.*

BELOW *The museum of wine taps at Oliveda, Capmany.*

INDEX

Acknowledgments

I would like to thank Hilary Lumsden for working so hard to make this book happen; the entire team at Mitchell Beazley for putting it together so well; Sam Stokes for her wonderfully sensitive and thorough editing; Tory for her superb photographs. I would also like to thank both Torres and Codorníu for their generous sponsorship of the photography, for which they asked no special treatment within my text. In addition to all the producers featured, I would like to thank Rocío Alberdi, Andrew McCarthy, Sarah Andrews, Sonia Benito, Carlos Mora, Colin Davies (for his fantastic website on Galicia), John Radford and Jeremy Watson (whose books and advice have proved invaluable), Ana Gállego, Sue Glasgow, and Christopher Payne. Finally, to Peter, without whose patient help and support this book would not exist.

Photography credits

All photographs are by Tory McTernan except for those on the following pages: 12, 21, 22, 27, 30, 31, 38, 41, 44, 47, 57, 58, 59, 60, 61, 65, 82, 83, 90, 91, 102, 110, 111, 112, 113, 116, 128, 137.